IRISH SEA SHIPPING

PUBLICISED

IRISH SEA
SHIPPING
PUBLICISED

R.N. FORSYTHE

With best wishes

Robert Forsythe

TEMPUS

First published 2002

PUBLISHED IN THE UNITED KINGDOM BY:
Tempus Publishing Ltd
The Mill, Brimscombe Port
Stroud, Gloucestershire GL5 2QG
www.tempus–publishing.com

PUBLISHED IN THE UNITED STATES OF AMERICA BY:
Tempus Publishing Inc.
2 Cumberland Street
Charleston, SC 29401
USA
www.tempuspublishing.com

British Library Cataloguing in Publication Data.
A catalogue record for this book is available from the British Library.

ISBN 0 7524 2355 X

Typesetting and origination by Tempus Publishing.
PRINTED AND BOUND IN GREAT BRITAIN.

Contents

Acknowledgements

To Campbell McCutcheon at Tempus, a big thankyou for his interest and support. Likewise to my wife Fiona who, strange as it may seem, is easily as enthusiastic about the subject as I am. Nowadays we have to thank baby Clare too who cannot really understand why Daddy has to stare at a funny screen so much.

The copyright ambiguities surrounding this material are considerable. I have contacted and acknowledge the help and courtesy of the following interested organisations: British Railways Board (Residuary) Ltd, National Railway Museum, Stena Line, Irish Ferries, Sea Containers and P&O. Should anyone feel I have infringed their interests, I am sorry and I plead indulgence.

The material shown, which is almost all from the Robert N. Forsythe collection, has been collected from many sources and it is usually invidious to single out individual contributors. However, not only has John Batts provided significant amounts of the older material but he took on the task of undertaking a proof read of the manuscript through a strangers eye which is a job well worth a thank you. Greg Norden contributed the carriage prints to our collection and Mr & Mrs McMurray the poster of the Mountains of Mourne.

Note

This is primarily an historical work. Change takes place with great rapidity and it should be noted that the text endeavours to be correct as at the end of 2001.

Introduction

The publication in 2000 of *To Western Scottish Waters* was something of a gamble by author and publisher. A book that allowed itself to be dominated by the sales publicity of shipping was an innovation. Thankfully the buying public appreciated the angle and this has led directly to the present volume. The thread of this book is the publicity that relates to shipping in the Irish Sea. Largely this means the ferry services between the nations that fringe the Irish Sea, it enables the Firth of Clyde and other Scottish ports to be prominent but the tale continues much further south and ultimately reaches round to Swansea. There is scope to look at some more local pleasure services active in the area and, of course, the Isle of Man, the island nation at the heart of the Irish Sea, has a role.

Very largely, this is a personal look at the subject revolving around the material in the author's collection. It means historical postcards and more recent pictures complement the publicity material. It also means that the account is located firmly within the twentieth century and within that there is a strong preponderance of items produced between 1950 and 1980. As it happens, this was a period of immense change for these services. The traditional passenger only steam packet was turned into the roll on/roll off diesel car ferry, and in the very recent past into the High Speed Superferry of various sorts. The classic bridge amidships coaster carrying cargo has been turned into a container carrier and that too is shown.

At least until the privatisation upheavals from the 1980s, the tale was largely dominated by four players. The **Isle of Man Steam Packet Company** looked after its own island before joining what are now the considerable interests in the Irish Sea of Sea Containers. Various British railway companies (including the pre-1922 Glasgow & South Western, the Lancashire & Yorkshire, the London & North Western, the Midland and the Great Western) had developed their own services and ports that ultimately became part of **British Railways** and thence Sealink and via various rebrandings/sales survive lineally today with Stena Line. A large and long lived holding company called **Coast Lines** incorporated well known concerns like the City of Cork Steam Packet, Belfast Steamship Company, British & Irish and Burns & Laird. Certain remains of that are now a part of P&O, who additionally via another history of take-over, working back through Townsend Thoresen and then the Atlantic Steam Navigation Company bring in routes from Preston and Cairnryan. One element of Coast Lines was sold before P&O involvement: **B&I** passed to the Irish Government and is today's Irish Ferries. That is only a brief summary, with yet other operators to be brought into the tale.

Journeys rarely stopped at the ferry port and whilst their extension by private transport is an unchartable topic the extension by rail and bus is a subject having much publicity which in some measure will be presented allowing such a famous operation as *The Irish Mail* to be appreciated from end to end. The depth of interest within this approach is revealed in three sub-topics which are each charted in detail. One charts the advent of the innovative vehicle ferries *Caledonian Princess* and *Lion*, a second reveals the chaos that the Britannia Bridge fire created, and the third looks at the competition the *Manx Viking* provided the Manx services with around 1980. Through these, there is the opportunity to share imagery which, whilst you the reader could seek it out, is frequently a neglected subject amongst the enthusiast and chronicler.

Selected Brief Chronology

1616	Donaghadee-Portpatrick given exclusive rights as an Ireland-Scotland ferry route. Subsequent growth of 'The Short Sea Route'.
1818	P.S. *Rob Roy* commences Clyde-Belfast sailings: first Great Britain-Ireland steamship service.
1819	Belfast-Liverpool steamship service opened.
1819-1820	P.S. *Talbot* first steamer on Holyhead-Ireland service and adoption by Post Office of steamers as mail packets at Holyhead.
1830	Isle of Man Steam Packet created.
1862	First Irish service from Stranraer.
1848	Commencement of London-Dublin *Irish Mail* train/ship service via Holyhead.
1904	Heysham Harbour opened.
1906	Fishguard Harbour opened.
1909	Loss of S.S. *Ellan Vannin*.
1916	Loss of T.S.S. *Connemara*.
1917	Advent of Coast Lines.
1920	City of Dublin Steam Packet Co. loses *Irish Mails* contract to London & North Western Railway.
1929	T.S.M.V. *Ulster Monarch* into service: first Irish Sea passenger motorship and first of thirteen 'Standard' Coast Lines vessels.
1948	Atlantic Steam Navigation open Preston-Larne roll on/roll off route.
1953	Loss of M.V. *Princess Victoria*.
1961	Advent of T.S.S. *Caledonian Princess*.
1965	Coast Lines sells B&I to Irish Government.
1970	Britannia Bridge fire.
1971	Coast Lines group sold to P&O.
1978	Manxline and the M.V. *Manx Viking* open Heysham-Douglas service.
1981	Cessation of Belfast Steamship Company services – by then P&O Irish Services.
1984	Sealink privatised: effectively the end of Irish Sea railway owned shipping.
1985	Isle of Man Steam Packet joins the Sea Containers group and their T.S.S. *Ben-My-Chree* is withdrawn. The end of regular Irish Sea STEAM passenger shipping.
1990	Stena purchase Sea Container's interests in Sealink services.
1992	First successful High Speed Ferry: Seacat Belfast-Stranraer.

CALEDONIAN RAILWAY.

LONDONDERRY, PORTRUSH, SLIGO, BALLINA, WESTPORT and DUBLIN
BY MESSRS. A. A. LAIRD & CO.'S STEAMERS
SHAMROCK, CEDAR, AZALEA, IRIS, VINE, THISTLE, ROSE, HOLLY and FERN.

Passengers going by Train from Glasgow to Greenock to join the Steamer there, travel from the CALEDONIAN COMPANY'S Central Station.

GLASGOW to LONDONDERRY.	LONDONDERRY to GLASGOW.
Every Monday, Train to Greenock at 7.15 p.m.	Every Tuesday,....................................at 6 p.m.
Every Tuesday, „ „ 7.15 p.m.	Every Wednesday,.............................,, 6 p.m.
Every Thursday, „ „ 7.15 p.m.	Every Friday,.....................................,, 6 p.m.
Every Friday, ... „ „ 7.15 p.m.	Every Saturday,................................,, 6 p.m.

Fares between Glasgow or Greenock and Londonderry (including Steward's Fee)—
Cabin and First Class, Single (including Railway Fare), 12s. 6d. Steerage, 4s.

Cabin and First Class, Return (available to return on any week day), including Railway Fare), 20s.

Cabin Tickets issued at the Railway Booking Offices at Glasgow and Paisley. Return Tickets (not transferable) are issued, available for Two Calendar Months from date of issue. Passengers may return per Messrs. Burns' Steamers. leaving Londonderry every Monday and Thursday. Passengers through-booked to Omagh, Enniskillen, Ballyshannon, Bundoran and Strabane.
Fares between Edinburgh and Londonderry—
First Class and Cabin—Single, 18s.; Return, 29s. 6d. Third Class and Steerage—6s. 6d.
Return Tickets available for Two Months.

GLASGOW to PORTRUSH.	PORTRUSH to GLASGOW.
Every Monday, Train to Greenock at 6.30 p.m.	Every Tuesday,................................at 7 p.m.
Every Thursday, „ „ 6.30 p.m.	Every Friday,...................................,, 7 p.m.
On Friday, 16th July, „ 7.15 p.m.	

Fares between Glasgow or Greenock and Portrush—
Cabin, 10s.; Return, available for Two Months, 15s.; Steerage, 3s. 6d.; Return, 6s.
Fares between Edinburgh and Portrush—
First Class and Cabin—Single, 15s. 6d.; Return, 24s. 6d. Third Class and Steerage—6s.
Return Tickets available for Two Months.

GLASGOW to BALLINA.	BALLINA to GLASGOW.
(With liberty to call at Sligo and Westport.)	(With liberty to call at Sligo.)
Tuesday, 6th July, Train to Greenock at 4 p.m.	Friday, 9th July, ...at 5 p.m.
Tuesday, 3rd August. „ „ 4 p.m.	

GLASGOW to WESTPORT.	WESTPORT to GLASGOW.
(With liberty to call at Sligo.)	(With liberty to call at Sligo and Ballina.)
Tuesday, 13th July, Train to Greenock at 4 p.m.	Friday, 2nd July, ...at 12 noon.
Tuesday, 27th „ „ „ 4 p.m.	Friday, 16th „ ....,, 10 a.m.
	Friday, 30th „ ....,, 10 a.m.

GLASGOW to SLIGO.	SLIGO to GLASGOW.
Saturday, 3rd July, Train to Greenock at 3 p.m.	Saturday, 3rd July, ...at 2 p.m.
Tuesday, 6th „ „ „ 4 p.m.	Tuesday, 6th „ ....,, 3 p.m.
Saturday, 10th „ „ „ 3 p.m.	Saturday, 10th „ ....,, 5 p.m.
Tuesday, 13th „ „ „ 4 p.m.	Tuesday, 13th „ ....,, 7 p.m.
Friday, 16th „ „ „ 7.15 p.m.	Saturday, 17th „ ....,, 12 noon.
Saturday, 24th „ „ „ 3 p.m.	Tuesday, 20th „ ....,, 3 p.m.
Tuesday, 27th „ „ „ 4 p.m.	Tuesday, 27th „ ....,, 7 p.m.
Saturday, 31st „ „ „ 3 p.m.	Saturday, 31st „ ....,, 12 noon.

Fares between Glasgow or Greenock and Sligo, Ballina or Westport—Cabin, Single, 12s. 6d.;
Return (not transferable), available for Two Months, 20s.; Steerage, 5s.; Return, 8s.
CARS leave SLIGO daily at 6.30 a.m. and 2.30 p.m. for BALLINA. and at 6 a.m. and 3 p.m. for BALLYSHANNON. Fares—Sligo to Ballina, 4s. 6d.; Sligo to Ballyshannon, 3s. 6d. N.B.—Afternoon Cars do not run on Sundays.

To DUBLIN, via GREENOCK.				From DUBLIN, via GREENOCK.			
	Train to G'nock. Cal. Rail. p.m.		Train to G'nock, Cal. Rail. p.m.		p.m.		p.m.
Satur., 3rd July	6 30	Thurs., 22nd July	6 30	Thurs., 1st July	6 0	Tues., 20th July	6 0
Thurs., 8th „	6 30	Tues., 27th „	6 30	Tues., 6th „	6 0	Satur., 24th „	4 0
Tues., 13th „	6 30	Satur., 31st „	6 30	Satur., 10th „	4 0	Thurs., 29th „	6 0
Satur., 17th „	8 0a			Thurs.. 15th „	6 0		

Apply to A. M. O'MALLEY, Westport; JOHN M'CULLOCH, Ballina; JAMES HARPER & Co., Sligo; JAMES M'NEIL & Co., Londonderry; DANIEL FALL & SON, or JAMES CALDWELL & SON, Portrush and Coleraine; WELLS & HOLOHAN, 9 North Wall, Dublin; ROBERT ALLAN & Co., Custom-House Quay, Greenock; and at the Offices of the Company, 7 North St. Andrew Street, Edinburgh; and 72 Great Clyde Street, Glasgow, to ALEX. A. LAIRD & Co.
For Through Fares to Dublin, see page 139.
For Through Fares to Dublin, see page 139.
For Sailings in AUGUST and SEPTEMBER, see the Steamboat Company's Monthly Bills, to be had at Railway Stations and Steam Packet Company's Offices.

One

Out of the Firth of Clyde

Glasgow represents one end of this tour which will make its way to Swansea. Beyond the needs of geography, Glasgow supplies another excellent reason to be the port of origin. Commercial steam boat operation had commenced with the P.S. *Comet* on the Clyde in 1812. Services mushroomed quickly and the first steamship service across the Irish Sea was started out of the Clyde in 1818 with the P.S. *Rob Roy*.

The pioneer was owned by David Napier and built in a yard which later became Denny's of Dumbarton, the builder of many of this volume's vessels. *Rob Roy* opened the Greenock–Belfast route so becoming the first regular cross-channel steamship operation anywhere in the world.

The Burns name had appeared on the route in 1826 and despite much early competition Burns prospered so well that nearly 100 years later they were part of the Coast Lines group who merged the company in 1922 to create the Burns & Laird Lines. Since 1851 Burns had had an absolute monopoly on the Scottish shipping routes from Belfast.

Survival of any nineteenth century publicity for these concerns will be exceptional outside a few institutional archives. Some sources available to us are the 1880 Tourist Programmes of the Caledonian Railway.

A series of whole page adverts detailed the connections between Scotland and Ireland. The page reproduced opposite shows the detail of the Laird line operations. At that time they were unconnected to Burns, but whilst Burns focussed on the Belfast route, Laird's offered connections to a number of other ports. That to Londonderry lasted longest and will be encountered again.

Irish Sea shipping should by no means be considered just as cross channel services with Ireland. There were and are 'domestic' passenger routes within the Irish Sea. In their own category are the Manx routes. Although the focus of Manx shipping is with passages to Liverpool and Heysham, all sorts of other links have existed. Even in the 1990s, there was an annual sailing to the island from a port as insignificant as Garlieston.

Scottish links to the island existed from a range of ports in the Firth of Clyde although Ardrossan was the most relied upon port latterly. In 1880 the Isle of Man Steam Packet operated the link via Greenock (see overleaf p.12). Around that time Caird's of Greenock was a favoured builder for Manx steam packets.

The extracts from the North British Railway timetable of July 1900 (pages 13 & 14) show a variety of routes. A whole page is given to the Burns service then available from Glasgow, Greenock and Ardrossan.

The Ayr services were rather marginal. They did not exist after 1936. From 1908 the Ayr company had been absorbed into Laird Lines. The Belfast service had started in 1889. On a daily basis it operated from later in 1900 until the First World War.

It will be seen that the Manx steamer started at Ardrossan three times a week with the Wednesday sailing from Scotland extended up the firth to include both Glasgow and Greenock.

DOUGLAS (ISLE OF MAN),
Via GREENOCK.

The Isle of Man Steam-Packet Coy.'s Steamer
LEAVES

GREENOCK for DOUGLAS (Isle of Man)
EVERY THURSDAY,

In connection with the following Trains—

4.30 p.m. from LEITH (Cal.).
5.0 p.m. from EDINBURGH (Princes Street).
6.30 p.m. from GLASGOW (Central).

It leaves DOUGLAS (Isle of Man) for GREENOCK every WEDNESDAY, at such times as tides may permit.

RETURN TICKETS AVAILABLE FOR TWO MONTHS,

FARES:—

	SINGLE.		RETURN.			SINGLE.		RETURN.	
	1 Cl. and Cabin.	3 Cl. and St'ge.	1 Cl. and Cabin.	3 Cl. and St'ge.		1 Cl. and Cabin.	3 Cl. and St'ge.	1 Cl. and Cabin.	3 Cl. and St'ge.
	s. d.	s. d.	s. d.	s. d.		s. d.	s. d.	s. d.	s. d
Aberdeen,	36 9	18 5	49 5	24 10	Forfar,	27 8	13 7½	37 6	18 10
Arbroath,	27 11	14 0½	38 4	19 5	Glasgow,	11 8	5 9	17 6	9 0
Alloa (North),	16 4	8 3½	23 10	12 2	Hamilton,	12 8	6 4½	19 6	10 3
Callander,	18 3	9 6	26 3	13 8	Leith,	16 9	8 3	27 0	13 0
Crieff,	20 9	10 4½	29 5	14 10	Montrose,	30 9	15 5	41 11	21 1
Dumfries,	24 9	12 4	39 7	19 9	Paisley,	11 8	5 9	17 6	9 0
Dundee,	25 8	12 7½	35 6	17 7	Perth,	21 9	10 11½	30 8	15 6
Edinburgh,	16 9	8 3	27 0	13 0	Stirling,	16 8	8 2	23 9	12 0

AYR STEAM SHIPPING COMPANY. 127
AYR AND BELFAST, AND AYR AND LARNE.
INCREASED BELFAST SERVICE.

SCOTLAND to IRELAND.	Monday, Wednesday, and Friday.	Monday, Tuesday, Thursday, and Saturday.	IRELAND to SCOTLAND.	Mon., Tues., Wed. and Fri.	Tues and Thur	Sat.
	p.m.	p.m.		p.m.	p.m.	p.m.
Train from Glasgow (St Enoch Station)	10 20	10 20	Steamer from Larne	...	9 0	6 *0
Steamer from Ayr	12 m0	12 m0	Steamer from Belfast	8 0	...	...
	a.m	a.m.		a.m.	a.m.	
,, Arrives at Belfast ... about	...	5 30	Train from Ayr	6 0	6 0	...
,, ,, at Larne ,, ,,	7 30	......	,, Arrives at Glasgow (St Enoch Stn.)	7 40	7 40	...

Passengers booked through from the principal Stations on the North British Railway
* No Train connection beyond Ayr on Sundays.

THE DUBLIN & GLASGOW STEAM PACKET COMPANY'S FIRST-CLASS STEAMSHIPS—"DUKE LINE."
(Calling at Greenock, Saturday's Steamer from Dublin excepted.)

GLASGOW to DUBLIN.		July	From Broomielaw.	DUBLIN to GLASGOW.			July	
Monday ...	... ...	2	2 0 p.m.	Monday ...	...	...	2	6 0 p.m.
Wednesday	... ...	4	2 0 ,,	Tuesday ...	...	...	3	6 0 ,,
Thursday ...	... ...	5	2 0 ,,	Wednesday...	...	...	4	6 0 ,,
Friday ...	... ...	6	2 0 ,,	Friday ...	...	...	6	6 0 ,,
Monday ...	... ...	9	2 0 ,,	Saturday ...	...	...	7	6 0 ,,
Tuesday ...	... ...	10	2 0 ,,	Monday ...	...	...	9	6 0 ,,
Wednesday	... ...	11	2 0 ,,	Wednesday	...	...	11	6 0 ,,
Friday ...	... ...	13	2 0 ,,	Thursday ...	...	...	12	6 0 ,,
Saturday ...	... ...	14	2 0 ,,	Friday ...	...	...	13	6 0 ,,
Monday ...	... ...	16	2 0 ,,	Monday ...	...	...	16	6 0 ,,
Wednesday	... ...	18	2 0 ,,	Tuesday ...	...	...	17	6 0 ,,
Thursday ...	... ...	19	2 0 ,,	Wednesday	...	...	18	6 0 ,,
Friday ...	... ...	20	2 0 ,,	Friday ...	...	...	20	6 0 ,,
Monday ...	... ...	23	2 0 ,,	Saturday ...	...	...	21	6 0 ,,
Tuesday ...	... ...	24	2 0 ,,	Monday ...	...	...	23	6 0 ,
Wednesday	... ...	25	2 0 ,,	Wednesday	...	...	25	6 0 ,,
Friday ...	... ...	27	2 0 ,,	Thursday ...	...	...	26	6 0 ,,
Saturday ...	... ...	28	2 0 ,,	Friday ...	...	...	27	6 0 ,,
Monday ...	... ...	30	2 0 ,,	Monday ...	...	...	30	6 0 ,,
				Tuesday ...	...	...	31	6 0 ,,

Train from Edinburgh (Waverley) at 4-0 p.m. and North Leith at 3-30 p.m. to Glasgow (Queen Street). Train from Glasgow (St Enoch) at 6-5 p.m., and due Greenock (Lynedoch Street) at 6-54 p.m.

Passengers conveyed by Omnibus from Queen Street Station to St Enoch Station in Glasgow.

Usual Sailing Hour from Greenock, **7-30 p.m** | H. LAMONT, Agent, 70 Wellington Street, Glasgow.

Messrs ALEX. A. LAIRD & CO.'S Glasgow and Dublin DIRECT Steamers (calling at Greenock, Custom House Quay, both ways).

GLASGOW to DUBLIN.		July	From Broomielaw.	DUBLIN to GLASGOW (Broomielaw).			July	
Tuesday	... ...	3	2 p.m.	Tuesday ...	...	...	3	5 0 p.m.
Thursday	... ...	5	2 ,,	Thursday ..	...	...	5	6 0 ,,
Saturday	... ...	7	2 ,,	Saturday ...	...	...	7	6 0 ,,
Tuesday	... ...	10	2 ,,	Tuesday ...	...	...	10	6 0 ,,
Thursday	... ...	12	2 ,,	Thursday ...	...	...	12	6 0 ,,
Saturday	... ...	14	2 ,,	Saturday ...	...	...	14	6 0 ,,
Tuesday	... ...	17	2 ,,	Tuesday ...	...	...	17	4 0 ,,
Thursday	... ...	19	2 ,,	Thursday ...	...	...	19	6 0 ,,
Saturday	... ...	21	2 ,,	Saturday ...	...	...	21	6 0 ,,
Tuesday	... ...	24	2 ,,	Tuesday ...	...	...	24	6 0 ,,
Thursday	... ...	26	2 ,,	Thursday ...	...	...	26	6 0 ,,
Saturday	... ...	28	2 ,,	Saturday ...	...	...	28	6 0 ,,
Tuesday...	... ...	31	2 ,,	Tuesday ...	...	...	31	4 0 ,,

Train from Edinburgh (Waverley) at 4-0 p.m. and North Leith at 3-30 p.m. to Glasgow (Queen Street). Train from Glasgow (St Enoch) at 6-5 p.m., and due Greenock (Lynedoch Street) at 6-54 p.m.

Passengers conveyed by Omnibus from Queen Street Station to St Enoch Station in Glasgow.

GLASGOW AND DOUGLAS (Isle of Man).
(Via Ardrossan and via Greenock.)

From GLASGOW to DOUGLAS. Calling at Ramsey for Passengers only (weather permitting).		Mon-days.*	Wed-nes-days.*	Fri-days.*	From DOUGLAS to GLASGOW. Calling at Ramsey for Passengers only (weather permitting).		Mon-days.*	Tues-days.*	Thurs-days.*
		a.m.	a.m.	p.m.			a.m.	a.m.	m'dn't
Glasgow (Steamer) ... ... depart	,,	...	7 0	.....	Douglas (Steamer) ... ... depart	12 ‡ 5	8 30	12 0
Greenock (Do.)	,,	......	9 0	.....	Ramsey ,, ... ,,	...	9‡30	Fridays
Glasgow (St Enoch) (Train) ...	,,	11 0	11 0	11 0				p.m.	
Ardrossan (Steamer)	,,	12 no'n	12 no'n	12 ngt	Ardrossan ,, ... arrive	6 40	5 0	6 40
		p.m.	p.m.	a.m.	Glasgow (St Enoch) (Train) ... ,,	7 30	6 30	7 30
Ramsey ,, ... arrive	,,	6 † 0	6†45	6 † 0	Greenock (Steamer) ... ... ,,	......	6 0	.....
Douglas ,, ... ,,		7 0	8 0	7 0	Glasgow (Do.) .. .. ,,	......	9 0	.....

Passengers per Glasgow & South-Western and North British Railways embark at Princes Pier, Greenock.
* During GLASGOW FAIR HOLIDAYS, from Thursday, 12th July to Saturday, 21st July inclusive, all of the above Sailings will be suspended. For particulars apply to Mr H. LAMONT, 70 Wellington Street, Glasgow, or the Secretary, at Douglas, Isle of Man.
† Calls weather permitting only. ‡ Sunday midnight

126

SCOTLAND AND IRELAND.

ROYAL MAIL STEAMERS

SERVICE TWICE DAILY (SUNDAYS EXCEPTED)

BETWEEN

EDINBURGH AND GLASGOW,

AND

BELFAST, DUBLIN, &c.,

via GREENOCK (PRINCES PIER) and via ARDROSSAN.

To		Via Greenock.	Via Ardrossan.
IRELAND.		Daily, Sundays excepted.	Daily, Sundays excepted
From Edinburgh (Waverley Station)	Train	§6 40 p.m.	§6 40 p.m
From Glasgow (Broomielaw)	Steamer	‡5 30 p.m.	......
From Glasgow (St Enoch Station)	Train	9 5 p.m.	10 0 p.m.
From Paisley (Gilmour St. Station)	Train	9 20 p.m.	10 16 p.m.
From Greenock (Prince's Pier)	Steamer	10 0 p.m.	......
From Ardrossan (Winton Pier)	Steamer	......	11 20 p.m.
Due at Belfast (Donegall Quay)	Steamer	*5 0 a.m.	*5 0 a.m
From Belfast for Londonderry (B. & N. C. Rly.)	Train	¶ * ‖6 30 a.m.	¶ * ‖6 30 a.m.
From Belfast for Londonderry (G. N. of I. Rly.)	Train	* ‖7 30 a.m.	* ‖7 30 a.m.
From Belfast for Dublin	Train	S * †‖7 30 a.m.	S * †‖7 30 a.m.

§ Passengers conveyed by Omnibus from Queen Street Station to St Enoch Station, Glasgow.
‖ Passengers can proceed from Belfast by later Trains during the day if they choose.   **S** 2-0 p.m. on Sundays.
† Breakfast Car accommodation provided by this Train.   ¶ 6-10 a.m. on Sundays.
‡ On Saturdays at 4-0 p.m.   * Irish Time.

From		Via Greenock.			Via Ardrossan.	
IRELAND.		Daily, Saturdays and Sundays excepted.	Saturdays only.		Daily, Saturdays and Sundays excepted.	
From Dublin...	Train	*2 45 p.m.	* ƒ5 40p.m.	......	* ƒ5 40 p.m.	......
From Londonderry (G. N. of I. Rly.) ...	Train	*3 5 p.m.	*6 0 p.m.	......	*6 0 p.m.	......
From Londonderry (B. & N. C. Rly.) ...	Train	*3 0 p.m.	*6 0 p.m.	......	*6 0 p.m.	......
From Belfast (Donegall Quay) ...	Steamer	*8 30 p.m.	*10 0 p.m.	......	*9 30 p.m.	......
Due at Greenock (Prince's Pier) ...	Steamer	4 0 a.m.	6 0 a.m.	......	......	......
From Greenock do. ...	Train	4 20 a.m.	......	......	......	......
Due at Ardrossan (Winton Pier) ...	Steamer	......	......	......	4 0 a.m.	......
From Ardrossan do. ...	Train	......	......	......	4 50 a.m.	......
Due at Paisley (Gilmour St.) ...	Train	4 50 a.m.	......	......	5 36 a.m.	......
Due at Glasgow (St Enoch) ...	Train	5 6 a.m.	......	......	5 51 a.m.	......
Due at Glasgow (Broomielaw) ...	Steamer	6 0 a.m.	8 0 a.m.	......	......	......
Due at Edinburgh (Waverley) ...	Train	c8 36 a.m.	d10 36 a.m.	......	c8 36 a.m.	......

* Irish Time.
c Passengers find their own means of conveyance from St Enoch Station to Queen Street Station, Glasgow.
d Passengers go on to Glasgow by Steamer and proceed from Queen Street Station by Train to Edinburgh.   No Trains from Greenock or Ardrossan to Glasgow on Sundays.
ƒ Dining Saloon runs on this Train.

SPECIAL NOTICE.—Passengers holding Through Tickets between Dublin, Drogheda, Dundalk, and Newry, and Stations in Scotland, are conveyed by Omnibus "*Free of Charge*" between the Great Northern Railway Company's Station in Belfast and Messrs Burns' Steamer morning and evening, Sundays excepted.

Tickets must be procured before going on board the Steamers, no Tickets being sold on board.

Berths secured at the Company's Offices, 30 Jamaica Street, Glasgow, and 49 Queen's Square, Belfast   Servants in Saloon pay full fare.

Return Tickets issued to and from Belfast, and to and from the interior of Ireland and Scotland, are available for **Two Months** all the year round, but are not transferable.

EXTENSION OF TICKETS.—Passengers holding Return Tickets, and wishing to stay a longer period than that for which the Tickets are available, can do so by paying the difference between the Return Fare and the sum of two Single Fares.

First and Second Class Passengers holding Through Tickets can travel by Limited Mail Trains between Belfast and Dublin without extra charge.

Through Tickets (unless where otherwise stated), in cases where the journey is not continuous, do not include the cost of transfer between Steamboats and Railway Stations, nor between Railway Termini in Towns.   No allowance can be made for any Ticket lost, mislaid, or not used.

Passengers must take charge of their own Luggage.   Owners of Steamer not responsible for loss of, or injury to, Passengers or their Luggage, from whatever cause arising.

At Ardrossan (Winton Pier) and Greenock the Railway Carriages go alongside the Steamer

Passengers from Scotland to Ireland may travel to Greenock or Ardrossan by any Train during the day; and those travelling from Ireland may break their journey at Ardrossan or Greenock, and proceed by any Train during the day

Passengers holding Through Return Tickets are allowed One Week both going and returning in which to complete their journey and Passengers holding Through Single Tickets are allowed One Week to complete the journey

Dogs will not be carried by these Steamers unless accompanied by some person in charge, or secured in a hamper or other package, and they will only be carried at Owner's risk.   They will not be allowed in the Cabin.

The information in this Notice is compiled with as much care as circumstances permit, but it must be distinctly understood that no responsibility whatever is undertaken for inaccuracies or alterations.   The Train Services in particular are subject to alteration.

Passengers, Passengers' Luggage, Live Stock, and Goods are carried by the Shipping Company subject to the published conditions

ALL FARES COVER STEWARD'S FEE.

For further information apply to

NORTH BRITISH RAILWAY COMPANY,

The Managers and Agents of the other Railway Companies carrying in connection with this Route, or to

G. & J. BURNS { Exchange Buildings, Leith ; 49 Queen's Square, Belfast ;
{ The Harbour, Ardrossan ; Excise Buildings, Greenock ; and 30 Jamaica Street, Glasgow.

1953

Introducing

M.V. "Irish Coast"

"A Crowning Achievement"

Inaugurating a New Reign
of Luxury Travel in our
Elizabethan Era

A look now at the Indian Summer of the classic passenger packet on these routes in the 1950s and at the transition to roll-on roll-off in the next decade.

Burns & Laird had since 1922 been the name that was synomous with the Irish services out of the Firth of Clyde. As part of the Coast Lines group they had benefited from a standard design of ship. Thirteen sisters were built between 1929 and 1957 commencing with the M.V. *Ulster Monarch* for the Belfast Steamship Company. This was a remarkable testimony to the design.

The focus in Coronation Year was on the M.V. *Irish Coast* which appeared late in 1952 from Harland & Wolff in Belfast. This leaflet detailed her summer service from Glasgow to Dublin with a call at Greenock. In the winter she acted as a relief vessel.

The leaflet for this service in the summer of 1955 focused on the passengers and not the ship. A tremendous amount of such literature was generated and little will survive although the quality of what Burns Laird (as expressed on the leaflet covers but Burns & Laird in the address) produced can be shown.

1957's timetable for the core Belfast-Glasgow service was particularly clever. (*below* and illustrations 3/4 in the colour section) An emblematic Scotsman and Irish colleen oversaw the comings and goings of another one of the standard vessels.

This portrays the M.V. *Royal Ulsterman*, which with its sistership the M.V. *Royal Scotsman* maintained the service between 1936 and 1967. Coast Lines were wedded quite early to the use of marine diesels unlike fellow Irish Sea operator Isle of Man Steam Packet. Both ships were products of Harland & Wolff. They saw war service including the Norwegian Campaign and evacuations from St Nazaire in 1940; in contrast *Royal Scotsman* was a headquarters ship during the landings in southern France from the Mediterranean in 1944.

SCOTLAND AND IRELAND — INTRODUCTION OF SAILING TICKETS - SUMMER SEASON 1958

As a means of controlling the traffic at peak periods on all Cross Channel Services "Sailing" Tickets to and from Ireland will be required for certain sailings as set out hereunder:-

IMPORTANT NOTICE—All Passengers travelling to and from Ireland on controlled sailing dates must be in possession of SAILING TICKET, and no Passenger will be permitted to travel out of ROUTE, DATE or CLASS other than specified on the Sailing Ticket

CONTROLLED SAILING TICKET DATES TO IRELAND

	JULY													AUGUST							SEPTEMBER			
	Fri	Sat	SUN	Mon	Fri	Wed	Thu	Fri	Sat	SUN	Mon	Tue	Fri	Sat	SUN	Mon	Thu	Fri	Sat	Mon	Sat	Sat	Sat	Sat
GLASGOW—BELFAST [Direct]	4	5	–	–	11	–	17	18	19	20	21	25	1	2	–	4	–	–	16	–	–	–	–	–
ARDROSSAN—BELFAST [Daylight]	4	5	–	7	11	–	17	18 ‡18	19 †19	20	21	–	1	2	3	4	–	15	16	18	–	–	–	–
GLASGOW—DUBLIN	4	–	–	7	–	16	–	18	–	21	–	–	1	–	–	4	14	15	–	–	–	–	–	–
GLASGOW—LONDONDERRY	4	–	–	7	–	16	–	18 *19	–	21	–	–	1	–	–	–	–	–	–	–	–	–	–	–

* EX GREENOCK   † SPECIAL SAILING EX ARDROSSAN, 2 P.M.

CONTROLLED SAILING TICKET DATES FROM IRELAND

	JULY									AUGUST							SEPTEMBER			
	Fri	Sat	Thu	Fri	Sat	SUN	Mon	Wed	Thu	Fri	Sat	SUN	Mon	Thu	Fri	Sat	Sat	Sat	Sat	Sat
BELFAST—GLASGOW [Direct]	11	12	–	18	19	20	21	30	31	1	2	3	4	–	15	16	–	–	–	–
BELFAST—ARDROSSAN [Daylight]	11	–	–	18	19	20	21	–	31	1 §1	2 §2	3	4	14	15	16	–	–	–	–
DUBLIN—GLASGOW	–	–	17	–	19	20	21	–	29	–	2	3	–	14	–	–	–	–	–	–
LONDONDERRY—GLASGOW	–	–	17	18 ‡19	–	–	–	–	31	–	2	3	–	14	–	16	6	13	20	27

‡ TO GREENOCK   § SPECIAL SAILING EX BELFAST, 10 A.M.

For the sailings as above, no passenger (except infants under 12 months old) will be allowed on board unless in possession of "Sailing" Ticket.

ALL SAILING TICKETS ARE ISSUED FREE OF CHARGE.

PASSPORTS or TRAVEL PERMITS are NOT required for travel between Great Britain and Northern Ireland or Eire.

Applications for "Sailing" Tickets and berth reservations will be accepted on and from Monday, 6th January, 1958, ON PURCHASE OF TRAVEL TICKETS, and should be made to the appropriate address shown, GIVING PARTICULARS OF THE STEAMER SERVICE FOR WHICH THE TICKETS ARE REQUIRED. (Alternative dates should also be given.)

It should be clearly indicated whether FIRST or SECOND CLASS Tickets are required.

Postal applications for Travel and "Sailing" Tickets should be accompanied by appropriate remittance and stamped addressed envelope.

ANY PERSON OBTAINING A "SAILING" TICKET AND UNABLE TO USE IT IS REQUIRED TO RETURN IT PROMPTLY TO OFFICE OF ISSUE

★ LOCAL RESIDENTS ONLY

IMPORTANT NOTICE—All Passengers and their Luggage are carried subject to the Company's Conditions of Carriage as exhibited in the Company's Offices.

ALL SAILINGS SUBJECT TO ALTERATION OR CANCELLATION WITHOUT PREVIOUS NOTICE

SAILING DAYS AND EMBARKATION TIMES SHOULD BE VERIFIED AT COMPANY'S OFFICES

FOR FURTHER INFORMATION, Apply to—

Burns & Laird Lines Ltd.
56 Robertson Street
Glasgow, C.2
Telephone: CENTRAL 6301

Burns & Laird Lines Ltd.
2 Castle Street
Edinburgh
Telephone: EDINBURGH 32205-6

Burns & Laird Lines Ltd.
9 Donegall Place
Belfast
Telephone: BELFAST 23636

Burns & Laird Lines Ltd.
16 Westmoreland Street
Dublin
Telephone: DUBLIN 77345

Burns & Laird Lines Ltd.
14 Brymner Street
Greenock
Telephone: GREENOCK 20208

Burns & Laird Lines Ltd.
The Harbour, Ardrossan
★ (Daylight Only)
Telephone: ARDROSSAN 505-6

Burns & Laird Lines Ltd.
Princes Quay
Londonderry
Telephone: LONDONDERRY 2235

In what in 1958 was an eight-page brochure, there is particular value in seeing the entire summer programme set out. The arrangements for special sailings on peak July days are notable. Since the various routes used Lancefield, Anderston and Broomielaw Quays at Glasgow, a degree of care needed to be exercised in boarding ship!

Over several years either side of 1960 a leaflet like this existed. The cover may seem simple but it calls for comment. Prominent is the funnel design for the Burns Laird Lines along with a pennant for exactly that: the BLL logo. Those funnel colours can be seen in the previous leaflet but not in the one featuring the *Irish Coast* whose V shape funnel colours were that of the parent Coast Lines and reflected the policy of using the vessel as relief cover away from Burns Laird Lines routes in the winter.

'To and from Ireland with your car' or 'what a hassle' because in the 1950s demand was growing faster than appropriate technology was being introduced. Whilst it was not quite driving your car across a couple of planks (which happened elsewhere) to go on board, it did mean allowing the vehicle to be craned on board. That meant turning up at the quay up to four hours before sailing.

This timetable covered the three Burns & Laird routes out of Glasgow to Belfast, Dublin and Londonderry. On the latter the cars went by cargo vessel 'which may not co-incide with passenger sailings' as was helpfully pointed out.

The operation was not cheap, the single journey could easily demolish a week's wages. Then the passenger reached Ireland and John S. Smith was commissioned to portray the relaxing result.

FARES

DUBLIN and	SINGLE			RETURN*		
	1st Cl.	1st Class Ship 2nd Class Rail	2nd Class	1st Cl.	1st Class Ship 2nd Class Rail	2nd Class
	s. d.	s. d.	s. d.	s. d.	s. d.	s. d.
Glasgow ...	54 3	—	28 3	89 6	—	56 6
Aberdeen ...	90 3	78 3	52 3	161 6	137 6	104 6
Dundee (W.) ...	74 2	67 6	41 6	129 4	116 0	83 0
Edinburgh ...	61 11	57 4	35 4	107 7	101 1	68 7
Stirling ...	61 5	57 1	33 0	103 10	99 0	66 0

*—Available for return within three calendar months.
Through Fares with all Principal Stations.
TRANSFER Second Class to First Class—Single **26/-**; Return **33/-**.
Children under 3 years are carried free ; over three and under 14 years, half-fare.
 Above Fares are subject to alteration without previous notice.

GENERAL INFORMATION

Important Notice.—All Passengers and their Luggage are carried subject to Conditions in Railway Companies' Time Tables and on the Company's Conditions of Carriage as exhibited in the Company's Offices.

Frequent calls are made at Merklands Wharf, Glasgow, by the ship on arrival from Dublin, where Passengers may disembark if they so desire.

PASSPORTS OR TRAVEL PERMIT CARDS are NOT required for travel between Great Britain and Republic of Ireland.

Train Connections.—The departures and arrivals of trains shown in these tables are published for the information of Passengers. Every care is taken to secure accuracy, but this Company does not hold itself responsible for late arrival nor for any alterations or inaccuracies in the information given.

Dogs are not allowed in the Passenger accommodation. Kennels are available.

Luggage.—Personal luggage up to 150 lbs. (First Class) or 100 lbs. (Second Class) carried free.

Boots and Shoes.—Passengers are requested not to place Boots or Shoes outside Stateroom doors. Stewards will collect for cleaning and return to Cabins.

For further information apply to

BURNS & LAIRD LINES LTD.

(Incorporated in Scotland)

		Telegrams	'Phone
Glasgow, C.2, 56 Robertson Street ...		" Burnslaird "	Central 6301
Edinburgh, 2, 2 Castle Street (Corner of Princes Street)	...	" Burnslaird "	32205-6
Ardrossan, The Harbour ...	...	" Burnslaird "	505-6
Greenock, 14 Brymner Street	...	" Burnslaird "	20105
Belfast, 9 Donegall Place ...	...	" Passengers "	23636
Dublin, C.4, 16 Westmoreland Street		" Ladyships "	77345
Londonderry, Princes Quay ...	...	" Burnslaird "	2235
Heysham Harbour ...	...	" Raven "	73

or

227 Regent St., London, W.1	...	" Comfyships " Wesdo London "	Regent 6627

and Principal Tourist Offices

ALL SAILINGS SUBJECT TO ALTERATION OR CANCELLATION WITHOUT PREVIOUS NOTICE

January, 1958. M'C. & Co. Ltd.

GLASGOW DUBLIN

BURNS & LAIRD LINES LTD

John S. Smith did a considerable volume of work for Burns & Laird. Their publicity was in league with the other Coast Lines companies which appear subsequently in this volume (Belfast Steamship, B&I, City of Cork). A John S. Smith Belfast Steamship postcard is in chapter 4 which confirms a further commission amongst these sister companies. I know he also did work for the City of Cork Co. and a variety of work for British Railways, some of which was Irish related and is illustrated when Fishguard is reached.

His moonlit portrayal is likely to show the 1957 'standard ship' M.V. *Scottish Coast*. The leaflet is dated January 1958 for the 1958 season. *Scottish Coast* only worked the service for a year before the previously discussed *Irish Coast* took over. The two ships were largely similar but the funnel colours and design are (or should be) the confirmation of identity.

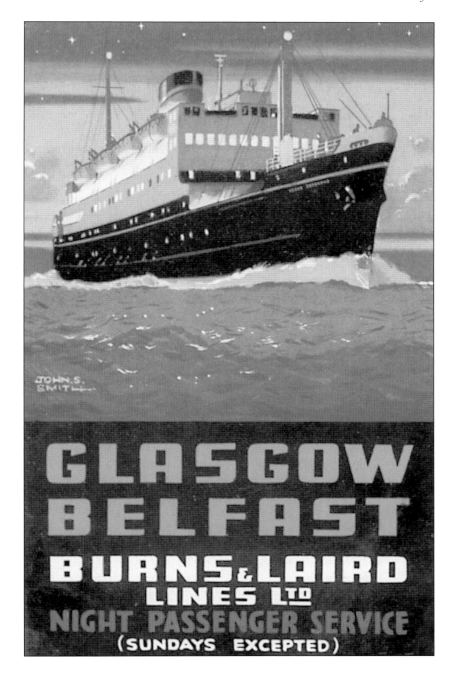

John S. Smith was responsible for another night image seen here – night because the core Glasgow-Belfast all year service was a night service. M.V. *Royal Scotsman* or *Royal Ulsterman* was the subject. It is quite possible that the artwork was used on several items for its exclusive use on what is a humble piece seems generous. This little four side leaflet was a 'briefing paper' handed to each passenger giving advice on what to do with your dog, how to get the steward to clean your shoes, etc. These leaflets could have a currency of some years. This one is undated but is known to be part of a sequence.

BURNS AND LAIRD LINES LIMITED

Glasgow & Londonderry

DIRECT PASSENGER SERVICE

23rd May to 30th August, 1958

With the object of giving a service which will make it possible to increase the carrying capacity on this route, it has been arranged to operate the m.v. "LAIRDS LOCH" entirely as a passenger ship from Friday, 23rd May, until Saturday, 30th August. The sailings under this arrangement will be as follows:—

From Glasgow at 6 p.m.—   Passengers embark between
   On Friday, 23rd May   -   4.30 p.m. and 5.45 p.m.
On and from MONDAY, 26th MAY, to SATURDAY, 30th AUGUST (inclusive). Three sailings per week in each direction.

From Glasgow—   Passengers embark between
   Mondays, Wednesdays and Fridays   -   4.30 p.m. and 5.45 p.m.

From Londonderry—
   Tuesdays, Thursdays and Saturdays   -   5.30 p.m. and 6.45 p.m.

On Friday, 4th July, ONLY the ship sailing from Glasgow calls at Greenock (Princes Pier) where passengers may embark between 8 p.m. and 8.15 p.m. Connecting train from Glasgow (St. Enoch) for Greenock (Princes Pier) departs 6.35 p.m.

The ship sailing from Londonderry on Thursday, 17th July, and Sunday, 20th July, calls Greenock (Princes Pier) where passengers may disembark if they so desire. All other Sailings DIRECT to and from Londonderry.

SPECIAL NOTES.

The sailing from Londonderry on Saturday, 5th July, is at 8.30 A.M. to Greenock ONLY and passengers embark between 8 A.M. and 8.30 A.M. The sailing from Londonderry on Saturday, 19th July, is at 8.45 A.M. (to Greenock ONLY), and passengers embark between 8.15 A.M. and 8.45 A.M.

For week commencing Monday, 1st September, there will be two passenger sailings in each direction, viz.:—From Glasgow, Wednesday, 3rd September, and Friday, 5th September, at 5 p.m., and from Londonderry, Thursday, 4th September, and Saturday, 6th September, at 7 p.m.

From week commencing 8th September the normal passenger service of two sailings per week in each direction will be resumed, viz.:—From Glasgow on Tuesdays and Fridays at 5 p.m. and from Londonderry on Wednesdays and Saturdays at 7 p.m.

ADDITIONAL SAILINGS.

From Greenock (Princes Pier)—   Passengers embark between
   Saturday, 5th July   -   -   -   8.30 p.m. and 9.15 p.m.

From Greenock (Princes Pier)—
   Saturday, 19th July   -   -   -   8.30 p.m. and 9.15 p.m.

From Glasgow—
   Sunday, 3rd August   -   -   -   6.30 A.M. and 7 A.M.

From Londonderry—
   Sunday, 6th July   -   -   -   -   5.30 p.m. and 6.45 p.m.

From Londonderry—
   Sunday, 20th July   -   -   -   -   5.30 p.m. and 6.45 p.m

From Londonderry—
   Sunday, 3rd August   -   -   -   7.30 p.m. and 8.45 p.m.

ALL SAILINGS SUBJECT TO ALTERATION OR CANCELLATION WITHOUT PREVIOUS NOTICE.

See other side.

Like the railways of the period, the shipping lines often relied on plain paper handbills. These may have little artistic appeal but can remain significant for their content.

This is the case with this handbill whose message is self-explanatory. M.V. *Lairds Loch* was a motor vessel which handled the service between 1944-1966, helped out in the summer by a cargo vessel. The only motor vessel regularly used on the service, she closed the route and ended up in Israeli hands.

There are stong links between Glasgow and the West of Ireland and additionally at times direct services linked Derry to Fleetwood, Liverpool and Heysham. Livestock was always carried in far greater numbers than humans but come the Glasgow Fair and there was a mass exodus of people going 'home' to Donegal and the West. The folk song *Free and Easy* with its key lines:

> *The first place I rambled to was Derry Quay*
> *A few miles distant from Ballybofey*
> *The next place I landed was in Glasgow Green*

is eloquent testimony to how this service entered the Irish psyche.

Once the boat link was gone, bus operators moved in using the Larne-Stranraer route for the crossing. An example of their publicity appears later.

BURNS & LAIRD LINES LTD

SPECIAL DAY EXCURSION

1964 RUGBY INTERNATIONAL

IRELAND
v
SCOTLAND

at DUBLIN on
SATURDAY 22nd FEBRUARY

M.V. SCOTTISH COAST

Dep. GLASGOW – FRIDAY 21st FEBRUARY
EMBARK FROM 5.00 p.m. SHIP SAILS 6.30 p.m.

Dep. DUBLIN – SATURDAY 22nd FEBRUARY
EMBARK FROM 6.00 p.m. SHIP SAILS 7.30 p.m.

RETURN FARE

First Class	Second Class
78/-	**40/6**

FULL CATERING FACILITIES WILL BE AVAILABLE ON BOARD SHIP

FURTHER PARTICULARS FROM:
BURNS & LAIRD LINES LTD 56 ROBERTSON ST GLASGOW
or
YOUR LOCAL TRAVEL AGENT

M^cC. & CO GLASGOW

Another flimsy, but with evident interest: sporting occasions are often the prompt for special publicity and whilst plain in design, the combination of transport and sporting interests adds value. 'McC.& Co' reveals the printer as McCorquodale and Co.: the Glasgow printer who handled much of the railway's printing requirements and in feel this handbill is not much different from a railway item of the period.

For a very long time, small numbers of passengers found a different way to travel by ship from Glasgow to Ireland apart from the Burns & Laird services. About the oldest British shipping company still in existence is the Clyde Shipping Company originating in 1815. Today they are primarily a towage company but for well over a century from 1856 they figured in the Irish Sea cargo trade.

Cargo vessels often offered passenger berths, a phenomenon still possible in the twenty-first century and the Clyde Shipping Co. was no exception. For us the interest is that they regularly advertised the facility.

The postcard shown as illustration 1 of the colour section of this book is of a Clyde Shipping Co. steamer and it has a carefully chosen location. The passage between the island of Little Cumbrae (left) and Arran (right) was doubly appropriate as a setting because the company's telegraphic address was 'CUMBRAE' and the coasters were usually named after lighthouses or lightships.

There were sailings which started at Mavisbank Quay in Glasgow where ships like the 1927 S.S. *Fastnet* and the 1936 *Rathlin* berthed. A rather simple representation of *Fastnet* graces the cover of the brochure as illustration 5 of the colour section, which promoted a six day voyage (the ship's weekly cycle) serving Dublin, Waterford and Cork. The item is entirely undated but is probably 1930s in origin.

It is the notes that accompany such brochures that can provide some mirth. Note 7 inside advised that 'It may be necessary, after leaving Mavisbank Quay, to load bunker coal during the serving of dinner at 1pm. Passengers are assured that every effort will be made to remove all traces of coal dust from the boat deck immediately'.

By 1962, the company's coasting fleet was down to three vessels and the last Irish service Clyde Shipping handled was from Waterford to Liverpool. The Liverpool chapter contains an example of another operator's cargo/passenger service.

Down the Firth of Clyde, Ardrossan occupied a special role in Irish services, a regular freight service reaching the new millennium.

Steamers first linked Ardrossan with Belfast in 1841 but success really only came after Burns became involved in 1882. For decades the key was the rail connection at Ardrossan which saw at one time the steamers berth at two piers in the harbour to cater for Glasgow & South Western Railway and Caledonian Railway passengers. The rail link ultimately lost most of its importance and Coast Lines, as the parent company, decided to introduce the 1960s innovation of a roll on roll off car ferry to the port. Like the Glasgow route, overnight crossings had formed the core service, until their abandonment in 1936.

Our glimpses start in 1958. The daylight crossing was a summer only operation which from 1933 to 1957 had been the regular preserve of the S.S. *Lairds Isle*. This leaflet from the next year portrays the distinctive funnel markings of her successor the *Irish Coast*. What a corker of a cover, signed too, but not by John S Smith, instead W.T.N. preserves some anonymity. I guess this was intended as the view from Ardrossan South Beach.

Since most Burns & Laird literature (and only a snippet has been shown) was pushed to the 'night' concept in its design, the chance to offer 'daylight' designs for the Ardrossan sailings must have been a relief to the designer. This simple but jolly portrayal of *Irish Coast* passing Ailsa Craig was the result in 1963. The leaflet cover seems to have been used for some years. An example for 1967 is identical save for the change of the funnel to the Burns & Laird Lines colours of the *Scottish Coast* as opposed to *Irish Coast's* Coast Lines design.

M.V. *Scottish Coast* of 1957 saw Coast Lines begin to address the issue of roll on roll off. This 1966 leaflet is good evidence although the arrangements were cumbersome for the ship was not designed as a car ferry. The leaflet stated that 'A 'drive-on' ramp will operate on the '*Scottish Coast*' to load and discharge Motor Cars at Ardrossan and Belfast'. This had started in 1965 and the ship had had a lift installed in her hold which carried twenty-five cars.

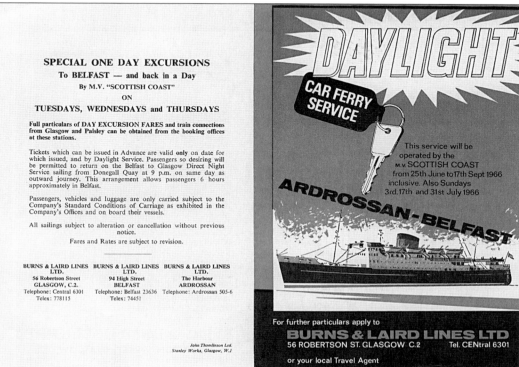

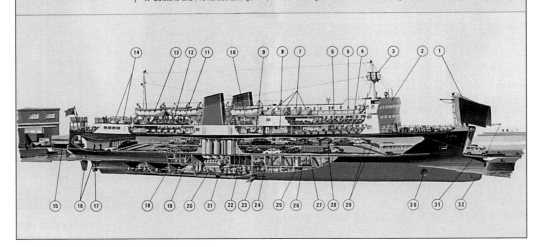

m.v. LION

1 Bow Visor Raised	12 Open Veranda and Bar	23 Stabiliser
2 Navigating Bridge	13 Lifeboats – 2 Motor – 4 Hand Propelled	24 Stabiliser Room
3 Radar Mast	14 Inflatable Life Rafts	25 Stores
4 Upper Deck Smoke Room and Bar	15 Stern Ramp Lowered	26 Crew Accommodation
5 Officers' Accommodation	16 Twin Rudders	27 Main Car Deck
6 Boat Deck Lounge	17 Controllable Pitch Propellers	28 Mezzanine Car Deck. Port and Starboard. (Can be hinged up to clear whole of main deck for high loads)
7 Inflatable Life Rafts	18 Engine Stores	
8 Main Entrance with Bureau and Shop	19 Gearing Room	
9 Dining Saloon	20 Main Engine Room	29 Hinged Ramps from Mezzanine Deck
10 4 Double Berth Cabins Starboard, 10 Single Day Cabins Port	21 Fuel Oil and Water Ballast Double Bottom Tanks	30 Bow Propulsion Unit
11 Cafeteria and Promenade Lounge	22 Lubricating Oil Tanks	31 Bow Ramp Lowered
		32 Bow Rudder

The new "drive-through" ferry ship

TAKE THE 'LION' ROUTE TO IRELAND!
New, fast, passenger car ferry and freight service

Scotland - Ireland

Whether you are a holidaymaker heading for the green, peaceful beauty of Northern Ireland, or a businessman hastening between important engagements, only the best is good enough in travel. Try Burns and Laird Lines' new ferry ship 'LION' which comes into service early January on the Ardrossan – Belfast daylight route.

Speed

Ardrossan was chosen for the Scottish terminal of the service because sailing time from there to Belfast is only four-and-a-quarter hours, as against nine hours from Glasgow. This is Glasgow's nearest car and vehicle ferry, no more than 30 miles away by road. Easy to reach from Carlisle too. For those travelling without cars there are special diesel train services which run right alongside the ship at Ardrossan.

Year-round service

No need to tailor your journeys in order to travel on certain days. 'LION' provides a daily service throughout the year, leaving Ardrossan at 10 a.m., arriving Belfast 2.15 p.m. On the return trip she sails from Belfast at 4.30 p.m., arriving Ardrossan at 8.45 p.m., in time for train connections to Glasgow, Edinburgh, Perth or Stirling the same night. In the peak summer months a double service is planned.

The NEW way to Ireland

Comfort for you . . .

Four de luxe cabins with berths, and a number of day cabins, have been provided for those who want to relax in privacy. There is a top-class restaurant accommodating 50 people. For more informal meals there is a self-service cafeteria. A central, all-electric galley provides the latest in catering facilities. Meals and bar service will be available at all times. Observation lounges, bars and a smoke room with television all equipped with comfortable seats, provide ample leisure accommodation.

. . . and for your car

'LION'S' hydraulically-operated bow and stern doors ensure maximum speed and minimum effort in 'drive through' transport. Vehicles are carried on the main car deck and on a folding mezzanine deck. A lift and stairways take you straight from the car deck to the passenger accommodation. Burns & Laird Lines Limited have been operating a passenger service between

Scotland and Ireland for over 100 years either from Glasgow or Ardrossan. The advantages of the short sea crossing are evident. There have been many well-known ships in their fleet, not the least famous being the 'VIPER' which made a name for itself on the Ardrossan – Belfast run earlier in this century. The name 'LION' is a reversion to the old custom whereby Burns' ships were called after animals.

Facts and figures

'LION' was built by Cammell Laird & Co. of Birkenhead. She is a one-class drive-through passenger vehicle ferry of 4,100 tons, 365 ft. long, with a 56 ft. beam, carrying 1,200 passengers and 170 cars. The ship is of all-welded construction and is powered by two diesel engines. She is fitted with stabilisers and has a speed of about 21 knots.

We could tell you much more about 'LION' - but why not put it to the test yourself? We are not afraid to claim that this is the best ship of her class. We welcome you aboard to prove it

The crude arrangements with *Scottish Coast* were repeated in 1967 (with a similar leaflet). Then in 1968 the revolution that British Railways had already achieved with their Irish services at Stranraer and with the Firth of Clyde services at Ardrossan itself was adopted in radical fashion by Burns & Laird.

The traditional all year overnight Glasgow-Belfast service was abandoned in September 1968 by when the new all year round car ferry from Belfast to Ardrossan was established. This had started with the new purpose built M.V. *Lion* from Cammell Laird's Birkenhead yard on 3 January 1968.

Lion was publicised both by its own version of the previous leaflet and by a twelve page brochure whose cover is reproduced as illustration 6 of the colour section. Doubtless there were posters and other memorabilia.

The brochure is quite spectacular. This was before colour photography could unthinkingly be used, Instead every page was illustrated by a commercial artist.

Lion seemed to get off to a very good start. For traffic from the Scottish central belt, Ardrossan was ideal. The sailing time was roughly half that of the Glasgow run whilst the narrow and twisty coast road beyond Ayr to Stranraer was avoided.

It was not to be. Three years later Coast Lines were acquired by P&O. Eventually the disturbances in the North of Ireland wrought havoc with the tourist trade whose cars *Lion* was meant for. In 1971–1973 (the example shown is 1972's cover) their two routes to Belfast were combined in one leaflet with the Burns & Laird Ardrossan service on one cover and the Belfast Steam Ship service to Liverpool on the reverse cover.

Both were in decline and after 12 February 1976 the passenger sailings from Ardrossan to Belfast were abandoned. The modern *Lion* was too valuable to waste and went off to operate with another P&O subsidiary from 1976. This was the Normandy Ferries' Dover-Boulogne run.

The Irish services and their timetables can be found in many sources, one (obviously) being the core British Railway timetable in its regional and later all lines issues. The all lines 1976 issue had its usual slot for the service in Table 260; however the columns were empty and the plaintive notice 'Details of service unavailable at time of going to press' inserted.

With *Lion* gone, P&O turned the Ardrossan run over to freight, in which guise it went on and on. The freight was perhaps less worried when weather made Ardrossan unusable. This is a not infrequent occurrence. Weather had delayed *Lion's* very first sailing and on numerous occasions forced *Lion* to Greenock.

The picture shows the incumbent in the mid-1980s. On 11 January 1987 M.V. *Belard* was leaving Ardrossan for Larne. *Belard* served the route until 1994. Her replacement was named the *Lion*. The route was moved to Troon in July 2001 and the vessel that closed the Ardrossan sailings was the M.V. *European Highlander*.

Ardrossan was for many decades associated with three groups of services. The Burns & Laird Irish service has just been described. The Firth of Clyde operations of Caledonian Steam Packet and its antecedents and successors appear in the author's book *To Western Scottish Waters*. This leaves the Isle of Man Steam Packet. They had not always used Ardrossan and previously a glimpse of their Greenock service has been afforded.

However, it was Ardrossan which became the Scottish port most closely associated with Manx sailings. These were quintessentially seasonal holiday operations. Calls at the northern Manx port of Ramsey were a feature and this route, passing along the whole length of the Rhins of Galloway, thence crossing to the Point of Ayre on Man before hugging the coast to Douglas, could on a fine day be a most scenic experience.

For many years a leaflet in similar vein to the 1958 example (opposite) appeared. The service ran into the 1980s before it retreated to Stranraer and then expired altogether (as detailed ahead). There was a mid-1990s attempt at revival by chartering the Caledonian MacBrayne vessel M.V. *Claymore*.

BRITISH RAILWAYS

B 23517

SPECIAL NOTICE

11.30 p.m. SAILING
TO THE ISLE OF MAN
FRIDAY 18th JULY, 1958

In order to save you the inconvenience of queueing at Glasgow (Central) Station for trains connecting with the 11.30 p.m., sailing from Ardrossan on Friday, 18th July, arrangements have been made for the accommodation on these trains to be controlled by a SPECIAL CONTROL TICKET which will be issued free of charge.

Groups of trains will leave Glasgow (Central) at approximately 7.45 p.m., 8.40 p.m., and 10.15 p.m.

When purchasing your rail and steamer ticket for this sailing at either Messrs. Rennie & Watson's or at the Ticket Office at Glasgow (Central), you should indicate by which service you desire to travel when you will be issued with a TRAIN CONTROL TICKET for that service if still available.

Postal applications to Messrs. Rennie & Watson should indicate by which train travel from Glasgow (Central) station is desired and a TRAIN CONTROL TICKET will be forwarded with the rail and steamer ticket. In case the train of your first choice is already fully booked, you should indicate a second preference

If you have obtained a rail and steamer ticket for this sailing without a TRAIN CONTROL TICKET, you should obtain a TRAIN CONTROL TICKET by presenting your rail and steamer travel ticket at any railway Ticket Office.

Early application should be made for CONTROL TICKETS and you should only arrive at Glasgow (Central) station a reasonable time before the departure time of your particular train.

This arrangement only applies in connection with the trains leaving Glasgow (Central) to Ardrossaan, during the evening of Friday, 18th July.

B.R. 35000—JP—January, 1958.   Munro Press Ltd., Perth

Summer traffic after 1945 fluctuated enormously and both the railway and the shipping company knew well that certain sailings could load to capacity. This called for some form of compulsory advance booking or regulation ticket. This happened seven times in the 1958 season. The relevant sailings were highlighted inside the previous item in red.

Additionally it is possible to find railway-produced literature for this phenomenon since the vast majority of passengers at the time arrived at Ardrossan by train from Glasgow.

On the previous page is a handbill for precisely one of the sailings detailed in the brochure on page 29. That brochure reveals how the service which usually operated a few times a week turned out three sailings that Friday leaving Ardrossan at 10.30 a.m., 4.30 p.m. and 11.30 p.m.

Looking at the BR handbill reveals that to feed the 11.30 p.m. sailing, three sets of trains were operated. In addition to the sailings being red (requiring compulsory advance purchase of tickets), access to the trains required a control ticket.

It does not take much imagination to visualise the hectic scenes behind these flimsy pieces of paper.

It was fortunate to be able to match the Steam Packet and the BR 'takes' on the same event in 1958. Even nicer to have been able to show a matching ticket. That would probably be a collecting struggle so I am satisfied to show a ticket for the same sort of operation but a decade later.

The traditional railway Edmondson card was used (by both railway and steamer company). This is a railway-issued ticket which cost nothing and whose sole purpose was to regulate the number of passengers boarding the steamer at Ardrossan. A valid travel ticket was required and the precise sailing of 12.00 on 4 August 1968 specified.

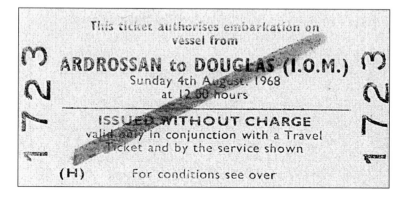

312	Campbeltown—Northern Ireland	VEHICLE FERRY

Western Ferries Ltd., Kennacraig, Argyll. ☏ Whitehouse 218.

	15-30 June & 1-17 Sept.	July and August	
	Fri., Sat., Sun., Mon.	Tue., Wed., Thu.	Fri., Sat., Sun., Mon.
Campbeltown	1000	1000	600 1400
Red Bay	1315	1315	915 1715
Red Bay	1400	1400	1000 1800
Campbeltown	1715	1715	1315 2115

Average Car Rate £8.00.   Fare 70p.

Between Ardrossan and Loch Ryan, down the Ayrshire coast of the Firth of Clyde, Irish sailings have operated from Ayr and Troon, the latter being a recent innovation.

On the western side of the Firth, Campbeltown affords a short crossing to either Red Bay or Ballycastle. From the Mull of Kintyre to Northern Ireland is a little over twelve miles though the port to port passages are somewhat longer. Unfortunately Campbeltown, although on the Scottish mainland, is a long way from any conurbation.

Since 1970 two operators have tried to make this crossing work using car ferries. Western Ferries with their M.V. *Sound of Islay* were first on the thirty-one mile route to Red Bay. This operated summer only from 1970-1973. Anyone with route specific publicity for this can count themselves fortunate. The author has resorted to showing how the final season's service was presented in the Highlands & Islands Development Board's late lamented *Getting around the Highlands & Islands* comprehensive timetable. It will be seen that the crossing at 3hrs 15 minutes was not fast and although two services a day were managed on peak days, one has to wonder how many people wanted to sail to Ireland from Campbeltown at 6 a.m. on a Sunday morning?

Ballycastle lies further north and west than Red Bay and the route to it from Campbeltown would need to hug the south shore of Kintyre to near the Mull and then cross the North Channel at its narrowest point before passing between Benmore or Fair Head and Rathlin Island, Ballycastle being situated in Rathlin Sound.

In the early 1990s, politicians and quangos played their part in encouraging a second attempt at a car ferry from Campbeltown. The route opened on Monday, 30 June 1997 with Donald Dewar, Secretary of State for Scotland, officiating.

Eighty jobs were created, £9.5 million spent on terminals, a Sea Containers subsidiary called the Argyll & Antrim Steam Packet created and a former Caledonian MacBrayne ferry, the *Claymore* of 1978, obtained to work two return sailings a day.

Many folk must have doubted the wisdom of all this and the service closed after the 1999 season. However the result is instant collectability for the timetable literature. I only know of a handful of items. The cover for the 1997 brochure is shown complete with a slightly and suitably doctored image of the *Claymore*. The 1998 brochure came with a cover slogan under the company crest 'A Journey into the Unknown'. I have always wondered whether the individual behind this had a sense of humour.

ARGYLL & ANTRIM STEAM PACKET COMPANY

Linking Argyll and Co. Antrim

Campbeltown

Ballycastle

ARGYLL & ANTRIM STEAM PACKET COMPANY

Tariff Guide 1997

Linking Argyll and Co. Antrim

Campbeltown

Ballycastle

Commencing in July 1997 a new ferry links the Kintyre peninsula of Scotland with Northern Ireland. Operated by a subsidiary of Sea Containers Ferries Scotland Ltd., the service joins Campbeltown in Argyll with Ballycastle in Co. Antrim. Its ship, the *MV Claymore*, will provide two round trips a day between the two countries during the summer season, and passage times will be just under three hours.

The service, to be known as the Argyll & Antrim Steam Packet Company, plans to extend progressively its period of operation from April to October. The MV Claymore can carry up to 50 cars and 300 passengers or 30 cars and two coaches and the same number of passengers, she also has the ability to transport freight.

FERRY TIMETABLE			
	DEPARTURE	ARRIVAL	
Campbeltown	07.00	10.00	Ballycastle
Ballycastle	10.45	13.45	Campbeltown
Campbeltown	15.30	18.30	Ballycastle
Ballycastle	19.15	22.15	Campbeltown

Crossing time 3 hours

For a brochure or more information call
0345 523 523 or contact your local travel agent.

33

Two

Loch Ryan, the North Channel and the Solway Firth

Although this account has started at Glasgow with the first steamers venturing into the Irish Sea, the crossing of the North Channel between Wigtownshire and County Down had a much older ancestry. Along with Holyhead and Milford Haven, Portpatrick was, in the early 1800s, one of the three British ports from which the mails went to Ireland and thus the subject of considerable government interest. A military road had terminated there by 1768. Traffic thence sailed to Donaghadee.

Portpatrick had a lot money sunk into it but was destined not to succeed in the age of the steamer. Despite the attentions of engineers like Smeaton, Telford and Rennie, the latter of whom created the impressive structures still to be seen, the result was too exposed for sail and too small for the age of steam. Steamers had succeeded sail at Portpatrick in 1825 but only lasted till 1848 when the Burns steamers at Glasgow gained the mail.

Portpatrick continued to see some services but it pinned its hopes on the arrival of the railway for a revival. The railway, complete with harbour branch, opened in 1862 but to get to Portpatrick it had passed Stranraer!

THE HARBOUR, DONAGHADEE.   R.910.

The revival at Portpatrick never happened though some desulatory sailings continued. At times of industrial unrest even in recent times, the fishing boats that still use Portpatrick have been known to carry passengers. The harbour was slumbering in the sun on 22 May 1989 (opposite).

The same tale occured across the channel at Donaghadee (above). Harbour improvements continued until 1863, the Belfast & County Down Railway had arrived in 1861. But by then Stranraer, Belfast and Larne were all preferred.

The result at Donaghadee was a magnificent harbour occupied by fishing boats and yachts.

Stranraer had seen its first steamship service as early as 1822 to Glasgow, in 1824 a service to Donaghadee was started. Regular services to Belfast commenced in 1835. These services were part of a very varied list of ports and they were not daily.

Rapid change came when the railway reached Stranraer in 1861, a year before it reached Portpatrick. When the railway reached Larne in 1872, the character of the Stranraer-Larne route became established, followed in 1878 by the creation of a fine pier station at Stranraer. By then the 1871-registered Larne & Stranraer Steamboat Company was in full sway. It was practically a subsidiary of several interested railways and it lasted (with some administrative changes) until 1923 when the LMS railway's creation brought all interested parties into one body.

Publicity for this early period would be quite a find in a shop today. Fraser MacHaffie's book *The Short Sea Route* managed by use of newspaper adverts and Scottish Record Office material to show some remarkable items covering these early Galloway services.

In their Edwardian heyday the Larne & Stranraer Steamship Commitee (as it had become), the linking Portpatrick & Wigtownshire Joint Railway and the Irish companies all produced attractive publicity, including posters, guidebooks and postcards.

A substantial example can be shown (pages 36/37). *Ireland's Enchanted North* is a 170 page guidebook published in 1910 by The Larne & Stranraer Royal Mail Steamers as then termed.

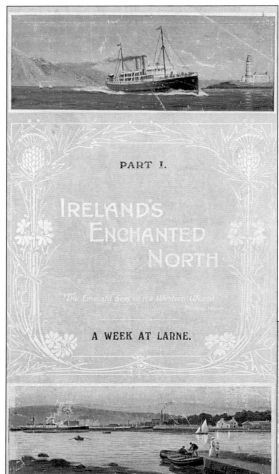

THE ROYAL MAIL AND SHORTEST SEA ROUTE
To and from IRELAND.

Open Sea only 70 Minutes.   Port to Port under 2 Hours.

Via STRANRAER and LARNE.

Summary of Through Service 1st May to 30th Sept., 1911.

To Ireland. | Light Type a.m. thus 10 16. / Dark Type p.m. thus 10 16. | **From Ireland.**

Trains run to and from Ship's side at Larne & Stranraer.

The Steamers are :—
"Princess Maud" (Turbine)—a Splendid Ship— and "Princess May" (Paddle Steamer)—very comfortable.

Additional Summer Service runs 12th June to 30th September.

A	B	C	D		Station		B	C	E
					LONDONDERRY (Waterside)	dep.	6 10	4 0	4 0
					Portrush ,,		7 0	4 25	4 25
					Ballycastle ,,		6 35	4 10	4 10
					Ballymena ,,		8 20	5 50	5 50
					DUBLIN (Amiens St.) ,,		6 5	3 0	3 0
					Drogheda ,,		6 47	3 46	3 46
					Warrenpoint ,,		..	4 15	4 15
					Sligo ,,		..	10 5	10 5
					Bundoran ,,		..	2 40	2 40
					Enniskillen ,,		..	1 30	1 30
					Newcastle (B. & C. D. Rly.) ,,		6d30	4 25	4 25
					Donaghadee ,,		7 50	4 25	4 25
					Bangor ,,		8 20	5 15	5 15
					BELFAST (York Road) .. ,,		9 5	6 30	6 30
					Larne Harbour ,,		10 0	7 15	7 15
					Stranraer Harbour ..	arr.	12 33	9 48	9 48
10 5	10 5	1 10	..	dep.	Aberdeen, C. R., Via Dumfries ,,		10 15	1 51	..
10 5	10 5	3 40	1 10	,,	,, ,, Glasgow		9 15	7 35	11 30
5 20	5 20	9g30	9g15	,,	Ayr		2 35	11 25	11 25
11 15	11 15	8 40	7h 5	,,	Birmingham, L. & N. W. Ry.		9 40	6 9	6 9
10 25	10 25	8h15	7h 0	,,	,, Mid. Ry.		9 55	7 25	8 35
12 53	12 53	10h45	10h35	,,	Bradford		6 25	4 10	4 25
4 40	4 40	3 10	3 10	,,	Carlisle		3 37	12 42	12 42
6 0	5 27	3 55	3 55	,,	Dumfries		2 50	11 59	11 59
11 30	11 30	3 30	..	,,	Dundee, C. R., Via Dumfries		8 45	12 8	..
11 30	11 30	5 0	3 20	,,	,, ,, Glasgow		7 19	6 35	9 20
2 5	2 5	6 0	..	,,	EDINBURGH, C.R., Via Dumfries ,,		5 45	9 30	..
[a25	[a25	7 5	..	,,	,, ,, Glasgow ,,		5 15	8 45	..
2 5	2 5	6 28	8 0	,,	,, N. B. R., ,, ,,		6 16	8 36	10 36
4 10	4 10	..	..	,,	GLASGOW (St. Enoch) Via Girvan ,,		3 45	12 21	12 21
2 30	2 30	9 30	9 30	,,	,, ,, Via Dumfries ,,		6 35	6 10	7 43
2 5	2 5	5 55	..	,,	,, (Central) ,,		5 55	9 30	..
12 27	12 27	10h28	9h40	,,	Harrogate, Via Leeds .. ,,		7 20	5 49	8 3
1 32	1 50	12h38	12h38	,,	Leeds, Mid. Ry. .. ,,		6 23	3 52	4 7
12b50	12b50	10 55	10h40	,,	Liverpool, Via L. & N. W. Ry. ,,		7b20	5 45	5 45
12 35	12 35	4 35	..	,,	,, ,, Mid. Ry. .. ,,		7 5	5 25	5 40
10 0	10 0	8 0	8f 0	,,	LONDON (Euston) .. ,,		10 45	7 10	7 10
9 30	9 45	8h15	8h15	,,	,, (St. Pancras) ,,		10 25	8 5	8 20
12c40	12c40	11 0	10h35	,,	Manchester, Via L. & N. W. Ry. ,,		7 30	5 25	5 25
12 30	12 30	4 35	..	,,	,, Mid. Ry. ,,		7 15	5 25	5 40
11 3	12 37	10 49	9l 37	,,	Middlesbrough .. ,,		7 47	7 22	9 20
1 18	2 55	1 15	1 15	,,	Newcastle-on-Tyne .. ,,		6 9	2 35	2 35
4 22	4 22	8g55	8g39	,,	Paisley (Gilmour St.) Via Girvan ,,		3 29	12 5	12 5
12 3	12 57	11h44	11h44	,,	Sheffield .. .. ,,		7 17	5 16	5 30
12 45	2 0	11 25	10 29	,,	Sunderland .. .. ,,		6 39	5 11	7 31
6 0	7 33	6 0	6 0		Stranraer Harbour				
7 46	9 15	7 46	7 46	arr.	Larne Harbour ..				
8 35	10 0	8 35	8 35	,,	BELFAST (York Road) ..				
9 25	11 20	9 25	9 25	,,	Bangor				
10 7	11e55	10 7	10 7	,,	Donaghadee				
10 50	..	10 50	10 50	,,	Newcastle (B. & C. D. Ry.) ..				
12 26	..	12 26	12 26	,,	Enniskillen				
1 45	..	1 45	1 45	,,	Bundoran				
3 55	..	3 55	3 55	,,	Sligo				
11 45	..	11 45	11 45	,,	Warrenpoint				
12 15	..	12 15	12 15	,,	Drogheda				
1 5	..	1 5	1 5	,,	DUBLIN (Amiens St.) ..				
8 51	..	8 51	8 51	,,	Ballymena				
11 7	..	11 7	11 7	,,	Ballycastle				
10 35	..	10 35	10 35	,,	Portrush				
11 0	..	11 0	11 0	,,	LONDONDERRY (Waterside)				

NOTES :

a—2.25 p.m. Sats.
b—Exchange Station
c -Victoria Station.
d—Mondays only.
e—Saturdays only; also Wednesdays and Fridays in July and August.
f—8-30 p.m. in June.
g—Via Dumfries.
h—Commencing 1st July.
l—8-28 p.m., commencing 17th Sept.

A.—Day Service to Stranraer.—Prior to 12th June and after 30th September Passengers to Ireland requiring to stay overnight at Stranraer may have Sleeping Berths on board Steamer at 2/6 each over Saloon Fare.
B—Through Daylight Service, every week-day from 12th June until 30th September. **C**—Saturday Nights and Sunday Mornings excepted. **D**—Sunday Nights and Monday Mornings only. **E**—Saturday Nights and Sunday Mornings only. Passengers to and from Stations on B. & C. D. Ry. and G. N. (Ireland) Ry. have to find own conveyance across Belfast. For General Travel Notes see next page.

The postcards covering the route exist in some number. John Allsop's *The Official Railway Postcard Book* tallies up around twenty pre-nationalisation cards. An entire album of Irish Sea packet steamer cards could be filled from the first half of the twentieth century which would be some task. The author recommends Allsop's well illustrated book as a means of appreciating just what was produced.

The postcard reproduced as the lower image on the first page of the colour section, appears to be a variant of an image Alsop catalogues as PWJ-191. The image is the same but the border design and text are different. The text makes no mention of Corsewall Lighthouse but thanks to Alsop's volume we can be confident that this landmark location at the mouth of Loch Ryan is intended.

Due to the note about an additional service on the reverse, it is clear that the card was issued in 1911. By then the Denny-built turbine steamer *Princess Maud* was seven years into her twenty-seven-year life. That ended in June 1931 when she ran aground at Island Magee near Larne.

Another aspect of Irish Sea publicity would be the related posters. Readers should remember that the intention of this volume is to illustrate what might still be readily found hence the stress on post 1945 materials and upon the smaller items like postcards, tickets and leaflets.

Posters have been collected for a considerable time and logically form the cream of a collection. However they possess two disadvantages. Storing and displaying any quantity is problematic. Before that, one usually has to buy them! Perusal of the annual Christie's South Kensington *British and Irish Travel Posters* sale catalogue is instructive. On the one hand magnificent posters of the ships by the likes of Leslie Wilcox or Norman Wilkinson, or of the landscapes by Henry Paul, appear as mouthwatering images. Then one checks out the realisations.

Whilst your author was busy building a collection for pence, other folk were paying £1,265 a go. That was the realisation for each of two Irish Sea railway steamer posters in the 1999 sale dating from 1935 and 1956.

One example of a related poster can feature. The posters tend to divide between those that feature the ships and those that use the landscape across the water to entice the traveller.

The Mountains of Mourne issued by British Railways is in the second category. It is a signed image of a small harbour (Newcastle, County Down?) nestling under the mountains undertaken by David Cobb in the 1950s. Cobb was a marine painter who also undertook for British Railways a number of carriage prints. The collection of the latter is gaining adherents providing a half way house between the large poster and the smaller ephemera that we concentrate on. A recent work by Greg Norden *Landscapes Under the Luggage Rack* explores this material. Relatively few such prints relate to our subject but C. Hamilton Ellis in 1951 did produce one of the 1860 Holyhead route steamer P.S. *Cambria* for use in London Midland Region of British Railways coaches. The M.V. *Cambria* and the T.S.S. *Duke of Lancaster* were also celebrated by the London Midland Region in this manner during 1957 and will be seen later.

The agenda of this book seeks to show how the humble ephemeral material can provide equal intensity of interest and as is about to become clear, the Stranraer-Larne sailings in the 1960s prove the point.

Never ignore the simplest handbill. Nowadays the high speed ferries mean most routes can offer realistic day excursion facilities. For many years, only the North Channel crossing could easily do so with special day charters being made from the mid-nineteenth century. In the era of the motor bus, linked excursions in both directions have been a feature right up to the present. They result in a variety of literature. This is a UTA-issued handbill from 1955 and it offers connections to Antrim Coast resorts specifically in connection with the key Scottish trade fair holidays. It is likely that these specific workings were to take week stay holidaymakers on to their destinations. Another regularly advertised facility in conjunction with a day trip from Stranraer was a train journey to the small seaside resort of Whitehead.

In connection with

GLASGOW, PAISLEY & KILMARNOCK FAIR HOLIDAYS

buses will operate as under on arrival of Steamers at LARNE HARBOUR

BUSES from LARNE HARBOUR to CUSHENDUN
(serving Ballygally, Glenarm, Carnlough, Waterfoot, Cushendall, Cushendun)

FRIDAY and SATURDAY, 15th and 16th JULY, 1955

LARNE HARBOUR depart :
9.30 a.m., 4.30, 9.10 p.m.

SATURDAY, 30th JULY, 1955

LARNE HARBOUR depart :
9.30 a.m., 9.10 p.m.

Fares :		Single
LARNE HARBOUR to LARNE BUS DEPOT		3d

LARNE BUS DEPOT to :	Single	Return
BALLYGALLY	11d	1/7
GLENARM	2/3	3/10
CARNLOUGH	2/9	4/9
WATERFOOT	4/4	7/4
CUSHENDALL	4/8	7/11
CUSHENDUN	5/7	9/4

**ULSTER TRANSPORT
Authority**

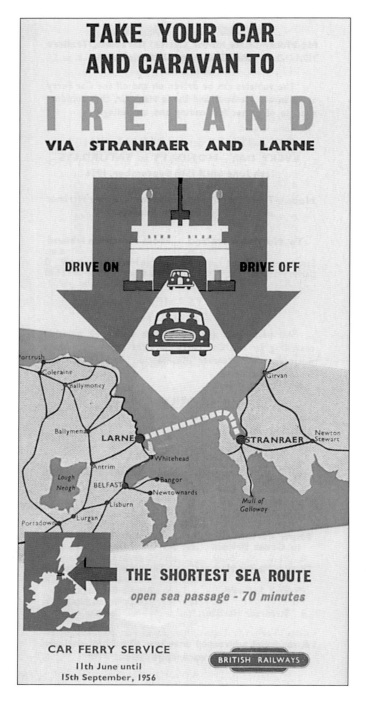

The accompanying illustration is of the cover of a leaflet that was certainly current in 1956-1958 (this is the 1956 edition). It was produced at a time when the route was in some flux.

Even before the Second World War the evident potential of a roll on/roll off car ferry service was recognised by the LMS. The route's second *Princess Victoria* had been commissioned in 1939 as a most up to the minute Denny-built motor car ferry. She operated the service for just two months before Admiralty requisition and her subsequent mining in May 1940 in the Humber. What price her publicity?

The LMS tried again in 1947 with the second Denny M.V. *Princess Victoria*. Her end in tragedy is well known when she sank with great loss of life, one casualty of the storms of 31 January 1953.

The loss of the Victoria was a body blow especially as the design was found to have fundamental failings. It was to be eight years before her replacement arrived.

Yet the demand remained, indeed there was even an air ferry in competition from Stranraer (Castle Kennedy) which carried 500 cars in July 1955 alone. To cope with the cars in the mid-1950s and use the expensive terminal facilities that the Victorias had had built for them, a spare ex-Southern Railway train ferry the S.S. *Hampton Ferry* was brought north each summer. In 1956 she carried 6,600 cars, a 120% increase in a year.

Passenger and Car Ferry Sailings until 17 June 1962
between Great Britain and Northern Ireland
via Stranraer and Larne
by new turbine steamer

Caledonian Princess

Caledonian Steam Packet Company (Irish Services) Limited in association with British Railways

It was not until 1959 and after much mithering that the British Transport Commission ordered the new ferry. When Denny's delivered T.S.S. *Caledonian Princess* in 1961, rarely can one vessel have received so much attention.

A lion rampant visible on her funnel in reality and in the publicity indicated a technical change in owner. To ensure that the results of the new ship could be monitored a subsidiary of the BR-owned, Clyde-based Caledonian Steam Packet called Caledonian Steam Packet (Irish Services) Ltd was brought into being. Their name can be seen at the base of the leaflet. The vessel took up service on 16 December 1961 and this leaflet was for the rest of the winter service.

ORDINARY FARES TO AND FROM NORTHERN IRELAND
(Liable to alteration)

SINGLE FARES WITH

From or to	LARNE HARBOUR			BELFAST (YORK ROAD)			LONDONDERRY		
	1st Class	2nd Class Rail 1st Class Ship	2nd Class	1st Class	2nd Class Rail 1st Class Ship	2nd Class	1st Class	2nd Class Rail 1st Class Ship	2nd Class
Aberdeen	99 6	76 6	62 0	106 8	81 3	66 9	134 1	108 8	85 0
Dundee (West)	81 0	64 0	49 6	88 2	69 9	54 3	115 7	97 2	72 6
Perth	75 6	60 0	45 6	82 8	64 9	50 3	110 1	92 2	68 6
Stirling	66 0	54 0	39 6	72 11	56 11	43 6	100 4	84 4	61 9
Edinburgh	70 9	55 3	42 0	73 10	57 2	44 3	101 3	84 7	62 6
Glasgow (St. Enoch)	56 10	46 8	33 9	59 10	48 9	35 6	87 3	76 2	53 9
Paisley (Gilmour St.)	55 9	46 5	32 6	59 7	48 6	35 3	87 0	75 11	53 6
Ayr	46 6	40 9	26 3	50 8	43 0	29 11	78 1	70 5	48 2
Stranraer Hbr.	29 6	—	15 0	36 8	34 3	19 9	64 1	61 8	38 0

RETURN FARES WITH

From or to	LARNE HARBOUR			BELFAST (YORK ROAD)			LONDONDERRY		
	1st Class	2nd Class Rail 1st Class Ship	2nd Class	1st Class	2nd Class Rail 1st Class Ship	2nd Class	1st Class	2nd Class Rail 1st Class Ship	2nd Class
Aberdeen	199 0	153 0	124 0	211 5	158 10	131 0	256 5	203 10	161 0
Dundee (West)	162 0	128 0	99 0	171 2	131 4	103 3	216 2	176 4	133 3
Perth	151 0	120 0	91 0	160 4	123 1	95 1	205 4	168 1	125 1
Stirling	132 0	108 0	79 0	136 3	108 8	81 4	183 3	153 8	111 4
Edinburgh	138 0	109 6	83 0	142 10	109 6	83 3	187 10	154 6	113 3
Glasgow (St. Enoch)	113 8	92 7	66 3	116 1	92 7	66 3	161 1	137 7	96 3
Paisley (Gilmour St.)	111 6	92 1	65 0	115 7	92 1	65 9	160 7	137 1	95 9
Ayr	93 0	81 6	52 6	98 1	82 2	56 0	143 1	127 2	86 0
Stranraer Hbr.	59 0	—	30 0	71 5	67 3	38 3	116 5	112 3	68 3

* **Notice as to Conditions.**—Tickets are issued subject to the Conditions and Regulations contained in the Bills and Notices of or applicable to British Railways or to any other body, company or person upon whose services the tickets may be available.

E.R. 35033/7 — R32605 — EK — January, 1962.   Printed in Great Britain by McCorquodale, Glasgow

NEW DAYLIGHT SERVICE

SCOTLAND WITH NORTHERN IRELAND

VIA STRANRAER AND LARNE

BY THE **NEW** SHIP

CALEDONIAN PRINCESS

SERVICES UNTIL 16th JUNE 1962

BRITISH RAILWAYS IN ASSOCIATION WITH
CALEDONIAN STEAM PACKET COMPANY (IRISH SERVICES) LTD.

T.S.S. CALEDONIAN PRINCESS

Caledonian Princess, 3,630 tons, is the latest and largest ship built for the short sea crossing between Stranraer and Larne. She is 353 feet in length, with a speed of 20½ knots.

The vessel was launched at Dumbarton in 1961. Like all modern ships she is fitted with the most up-to-date navigational and scientific aids, and stabilisers for added comfort.

Caledonian Princess has accommodation for 1,400 passengers. There are fine comfortable lounges, a restaurant, cafeteria, and two refreshment bars.

The ship has a spacious car deck with accommodation for more than 100 cars, caravans and lorries. Vehicles can be driven on and off at any state of the tide.

By CALEDONIAN PRINCESS
to and from IRELAND
– the DAYLIGHT SHORT SEA ROUTE

This is the matching leaflet issued in January 1962 aimed at the train service from Scottish stations via Glasgow to Belfast and Londonderry. Plain handbills issued from 18 December seem to have covered the interim period. A delay of some weeks in her original date of introduction (intended as 2 October 1961) may explain their use. Should anyone produce any publicity for an October start date, that would be some find!

The publicity became more dramatic from the summer of 1962. Full colour artwork inside and out in which such details as loading a Ford Consul, the ramp arrangements and the funnel colours appear. An image in this genre but taken from an imaginary aerial viewpoint and including more of the station and the loch formed a strong colour cover of the children's *Treasure* magazine in September 1963.

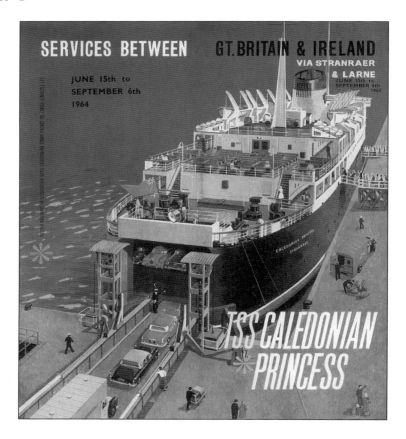

Throughout the first few years of her life, the *Caledonian Princess* received the most appealing publicity. In the summer of 1964, the cover was a subtle version of the 1962 one. The ship's name and port of registry have appeared, as has a Royal Mail van on the quayside to remind us that this was a mail steamer with the *kudos* that implied.

Different cars and lorries are on the linkspan and inside another image shows a Rover P5 pulling a caravan off the linkspan with the wooden building of Stranraer Harbour station visible. This latter image provided the cover in at least 1964 and 1965 for a purely car carrying leaflet. In those years traffic mushroomed with 56,000 cars being carried in 1962 alone.

1965 brought changes which were made apparent in the summer season leaflet shown illustration 7 of the colour section. Nationally, British Railways was adopting its corporate image which employed rail blue. Both this and the double arrow were usually applied to the ships. In 1965 *Caledonian Princess* gained the blue hull and this striking image of the vessel passing Corsewall Lighthouse appeared on that summer's leaflet. Corsewall is a most evocative place whether on a crisp clear day when Ireland, Kintyre, the Ayrshire Coast and Ailsa Craig combine to give an impression of a landlocked sea, or in a storm when it is possible to imagine the desperate hours during which the *Princess Victoria* wallowed in the seas off the point back in 1953.

The lion rampant funnel on the blue hull was only carried in 1965. To fully explain is complex but the essence was whether the dictat of the London British Railways Board headquarters or the local Gourock headquarters of Caledonian Steam Packet would triumph. Local management was almost proving too successful and when the vessel emerged from refit in March 1966 the corporate image was utterly triumphant with a red funnel and BR double arrows. From January 1967 the vessel was directly owned by the British Railways Board.

The scenes visible at the artist's hands are visible here at the photographer's hand in a view of *Caledonian Princess* in her first years of service tied up at Stranraer Harbour. The Ayrshire registered BMW Isetta bubble car helps the period piece. British manufacture of these was carried out in the former Pullman Car Company's Brighton works, a site lacking proper road access.

There is potentially much else to collect beside the core route leaflets. There were day and half day excursion programmes using the new ship from the soon to be closed Dumfries-Stranraer line as well as Ayrshire stations. Sports events and the July trade holidays provide more.

ADDITIONAL SERVICES
for motor cars
drive on - drive off

GREAT BRITAIN
NORTHERN IRELAND
via Stranraer and Larne
by M.V. "LOHENGRIN"

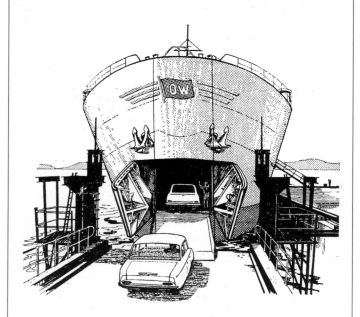

DAILY—MONDAYS TO SATURDAYS
JUNE 7 to SEPTEMBER 25, 1965

NOTE.—The Sailings shown in this folder are in addition to the advertised "Caledonian Princess" Car Ferry Service which operates twice daily in each direction between Stranraer and Larne throughout the year.

Growth was such that the new company turned in a 1963 profit of 48% on gross earnings, but the ship was the only roll on/roll off primarily passenger ship at work in the Irish Sea at the time. Something had to be done for 1965 and this leaflet cover shows the result. Caledonian Steam Packet (Irish Services) Ltd made clear that they were the happy promoters of growth!

The company chartered the Wagnerian-sounding M.V. *Lohengrin* from Bremen's Wallenius Lines between 7 June and 25 September 1965. This dedicated roll on/roll off ferry could carry 300 cars but no passengers.

She offered one return trip a day with passengers using the *Caledonian Princess's* two return sailings. This was all spelt out inside. It is unusual for publicity to so clearly identify a chartered vessel.

See this in the context of 2000 when Stena offered up to eleven departures a day in September to both Belfast and Larne from Stranraer.

Use of non–passenger carrying reliefs was clearly unsatisfactory. Prior to *Lohengrin*, BR's own M.V. *Slieve Donard* has been used. A new ship was hoped for but another solution was planned for the next two seasons.

No-one could have understood the prophetic symbolism of chartering the M.V. *Stena Nordica* for service from 14 February 1966 to provide two passenger ships and four return sailings a day. Stena's purchase of the former railway routes was still thirty-three years away.

The *Stena Nordica* ended up staying at Stranraer until 1971. She was mentioned by name in many of the leaflets of the period including a very simple one side flyer dated from 14 February 1966 which introduced her sailings.

The author only knows of one appearance of her by way of cover illustration which was on this winter 1966 leaflet whose other little nuances include the full C.S.P. (I.S.) Ltd title and Ailsa Craig on the horizon of the *Caledonian Princess* image. Simple one colour printing was quite a comedown from the glorious full colour artwork of the year before.

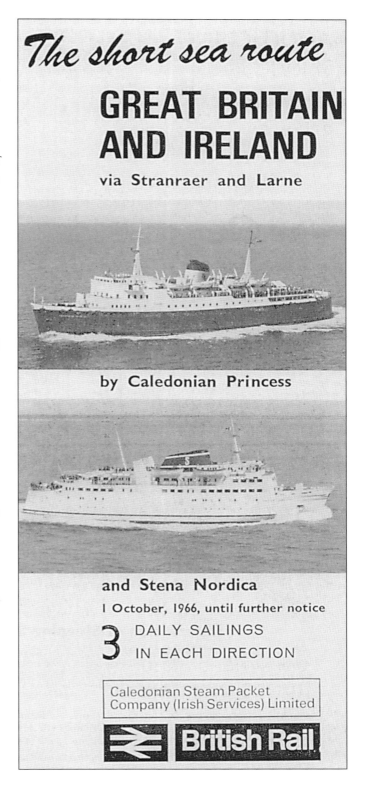

The short sea route

GREAT BRITAIN AND IRELAND

via Stranraer and Larne

by Caledonian Princess

and Stena Nordica

1 October, 1966, until further notice

3 DAILY SAILINGS IN EACH DIRECTION

Caledonian Steam Packet Company (Irish Services) Limited

British Rail

BRITISH RAILWAYS AND ULSTER TRANSPORT AUTHORITY

STEAMER CRUISE

TO

STRANRAER

By the Luxurious Steamers
"CALEDONIAN PRINCESS" and "STENA NORDICA"

On WEEK-DAYS

[Except Saturdays, during JULY and AUGUST]
From 2nd May till 30th September, 1966

One challenge in establishing a collection of this type of literature is that the collection will tend to be influenced by which side of the Irish Sea you live on. There are usually two sets of literature intended for each market and unless the collector frequently travels each way, full sets will be difficult to find. I freely admit that my examples of Irish-originated publicity are far fewer in number.

That makes it important to illustrate this example. A lot of UTA handbills have been seen but only this one for the shipping operations is to hand. It has to be said that even by the poor standards of the handbill, the UTA ones possess even less design consistency than the BR ones!

Irish designers were quite happy to borrow British Railways engines and here they used one of the three Heysham–Belfast route Dukes for inspiration. The promotion is for days out to Stranraer and, being 1966, *Stena Nordica* is named.

The new ship to replace the chartered tonnage arrived late in 1967, although come the following summer, it was *Caledonian Princess* that actually left for pastures new.

The M.V. *Antrim Princess* stayed at Stranraer until October 1985 when it commenced an association with Manx services. It is interesting to compare the launch publicity of the two Princesses, it has to be said that *Antrim Princess* comes a poor second. A few items featured her but they lack the artistic and commercial confidence of the 1961–1963 period.

This item (opposite, top) is part of the cover of her introductory leaflet, nearly half was white space and the artwork seems more like a concept sketch than a finished piece. It was the same inside. The leaflet is one of the last with Caledonian Steam Packet branding and soon afterwards a new brand appeared called British Transport Ship Management (Scotland).

This leaflet was purely an introduction to the ship and it managed to be entirely undated. What enables it to be so securely placed at the outset of the ship's life is reference in some detail on the back cover to the three ships of the route which named *Caledonian Princess* and *Stena Nordica*, a situation which as explained above lasted only a few months in 1968.

There's a new bridge to Ireland

— CALLED "ANTRIM PRINCESS"

Caledonian Princess had had her fame as the only roll on/roll off passenger ferry on the Irish Sea at her launch and as Denny's last British packet; she gained more fame at the end of her career. Aged twenty, 1981 was her last season for Sealink by which time she was, with Denny's *Maid of Kent*, the last steam-powered vessel in their fleet. Both were withdrawn within days of each other that autumn.

Withdrawn from Dover sailings, she appeared on the Tyne in overall white as a nightclub ship during 1983. For nine years from 1988-1997, she was on the Clyde in Glasgow but is now once again moored under the bridges at Newcastle and producing *Tuxedo Princess* literature for the collector.

This picture, taken on 28 June 1998, shows her in a temporary berth at Spillers Maltings, Newcastle, before re-opening. That sense of dogged survival that Irish Sea crossings demanded survived with the name *Caledonian Princess* in place on the port bow and with the twin lions rampant of the Caledonian Steam Packet still gracing her bow.

Earlier, mention has been made of the Glasgow-Londonderry shipping service and how until 1966 it played a role in linking families split between Donegal and the central belt of Scotland. Four years later and the publicity for the journey was now for a coach and ship service. One journey each way ran from Friday to Mondays making clear that the market was with holidaymakers and returning families. A similar leaflet for a route to the Donegal seaside resort of Bundoran exists. The cover featured one of Western Scottish's Leyland Leopard vehicles with the classic

Alexander of Falkirk Y-type body, a design combination that only finally left their fleet in 2001.

The story of the cross-channel coach services and their advertising could go on and on. There are a lot of leaflets out there and one or two more will be used later. In the 1990s a booklet produced by Ulsterbus was a regular and it included the Middlesbrough-Belfast service about which it is not easy to find information on this side of the channel. The route actually passes three miles from the author's home, not that I think that anyone else in the Tyne Valley would know of its existence! Latterly it has run for a very short season as in 1999. There are potentially years of individual leaflets to search out and, aside from timetables, establishing when such a service commenced and ceased would be some challenge.

The example shown below is for the 1983 route 349 summer service which ran for nearly four months around a long weekend pattern of one journey each way over four days.

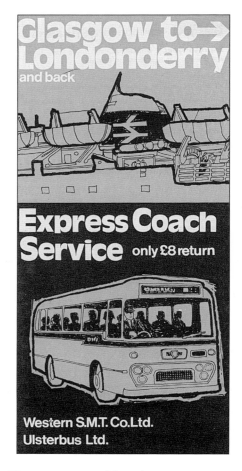

The appearance of three bus operators poses the question about exactly who operated what. In general it was not uncommon for the coaches not to board ships and for a connecting coach to appear at the other port. Ulsterbus even maintain to this day a depot at Stranraer in order to provide their contractual commitments and tours on the mainland side.

The leaflet is also unusual on account of the appearance of British Transport Ship Management. That must have been an anachronistic leftover that no one had noticed needed correcting. This company had really been another legal device in the London/Glasgow rivalry being operational from 1969. Another manifestation of it was the use of its initials on crew jerseys. Sealink as a name had much more currency and from what I read B.T.S.M. was not current after 1979.

The name British Transport Ship Management had appeared on certain Stranraer route leaflets in those ten years, generally for leaflets like those promoting the car ferry service that were issued from the Scottish office and not from headquarters. From 1970 Sealink was a brand widely used on the publicity material of the British Railways Shipping and International Services Division (itself created in 1968), although as a company Sealink was not formed until 1979 as a precursor of privatisation.

Throughout the 1970s, the route had received a highly standardised leaflet setting it in its railway context, examples from other routes will be seen later but they all shared a standard cover.

Then from 1980 Sealink, Northern Ireland Railways and British Rail joined forces to promote 'The Big Connections' for the route, a theme which was maintained on the brochure through that decade, whilst the actual size of the brochure expanded from one third A4 though a square format and on to A4 itself.

During this period, Sealink was privatised and the transition was well documented by these brochures. The double arrows on the ships' funnels only a few years before have gone, replaced by the generally white hull and Sealink British Ferries brand of the Sea Containers owned period which lasted all of six years.

Privatisation had not yet touched the mainline however, so the British Rail class 86 electric engine on the cover of the 1987 brochure carried the corporate blue.

Northern Ireland Railways were a bit more idiosyncratic and did not submit the most photogenic image although train 451 was a new Castle-class train built at BREL's Derby Works in 1985.

The ship itself was M.V. *Galloway Princess*, current on the route from 1979 and which has borne all of the BR, Sealink British Ferries, Sealink Stena, Stena Sealink and Stena Line colours, having become *Stena Galloway*. In 1980 she had featured with colour artwork on the route's car ferry leaflet.

Other forms of ephemera can help tell the tale, even a humble Edmondson card ticket recovered from the ground. The key point about the ticket (dated 30 May 1986) is in these words: 'Sealink (Sc) Ltd Seaman Ayr to Glasgow (Central)'.

What use did Sealink have for conveying seamen between those two towns? The explanation is that the demand for seamen by the various ferry companies at Stranraer outstrips the local supply. Glasgow is an obvious source but while there is a frequent train service to Ayr, that on to Stranraer is much reduced. Sealink therefore, as an ex-railway organisation had a deal to issue these tickets to get staff to Ayr and from there they used a contract bus service.

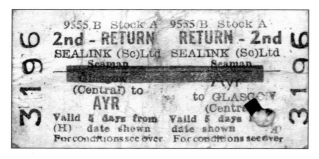

On 16 April 1990, the author was able to photograph the bus at Ayr. It was a Western Scottish Seddon of Stranraer depot (SS for Stranraer Seddon) which was specially painted in an overall advert livery for Sealink British Ferries.

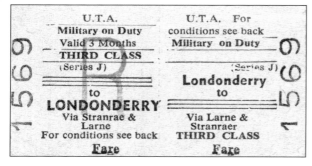

Incidentally good numbers of Edmondson tickets – the classic ticket design – have survived from the Ulster Transport Authority and Northern Ireland Railways. They are readily available from the Transport Ticket Society whose stocks include some cross-channel examples via Larne.

M.V. BARDIC FERRY

Although the railway ships in their different guises will always seem the mainstay of the sailings out of Loch Ryan, it has played host to two other terminals apart from the Railway Pier at Stranraer.

The Second World War created the second when an entirely new emergency port was built at Cairnryan. This never worked to full capacity. One of its piers became a scrapyard at which a succession of famous warships met their end including the carriers H.M.S. *Bulwark* and *Ark Royal*.

Another part of the port attracted the Atlantic Steam Navigation Company's attention in 1973 (a note about that company's growth is in chapter three). Since 1971 A.S.N. had been part of European Ferries. In image terms, this means that in due course Townsend Thoresen and thence P&O colours would become familiar on Loch Ryan.

Back in 1973 when A.S.N. opened the Cairnryan-Larne run it was under the brand Transport Ferry Service for which literature covering the route until 1974 can be found. Thence the brand Townsend Thoresen Car Ferries was used.

Although this was not so long ago, anyone with actual publicity for the birth of this service is fortunate. The nearest I can get is an official postcard of one of the ships used near its inception. The A.S.N fleet used the form _____*ic Ferry*. M.V. *Bardic Ferry* was transferred in from October 1974. This image probably pre-dates this for the ship came from Denny in 1957. Is the setting the ship on trials in the Clyde on one of the two measured miles at Skelmorlie or Arran?

Fifteen years on and the service was well established and in the midst of the image change between Townsend Thoresen and P&O. On 9 May 1987, it was Townsend Thoresen's orange which the M.V. *Europic Ferry* carried at Cairnryan. She had been at the port since 1983.

The two level linkspan and the freight vehicles on the open deck are evident.

By 7 July 1988, *Europic Ferry* had her P&O blue colours in this otherwise identical shot.

The vessel had particular interest in being the last Atlantic Steam Navigation ferry to survive in the P&O fleet. She had been built on the Tyne at Swan Hunter's in 1967 and finally left Cairnryan for Greek owners in 1993. In her last year wth P&O she had been re-named to *European Freighter*.

Her character as a stretched version of the Denny vessels like *Bardic Ferry* is clear.

In the 1986 and 1987 seasons, the Townsend Thoresen 'orange' literature made its last appearance. In addition to the nationwide A4 brochure which was similar in concept to Sealink's hardy annual, an A4 route specific brochure for Larne/Cairnryan was available.

The 1986 cover is shown. The ferry appears un-named and the shipping line's name on the side looks more like the work of the graphic artist than the shipyard painter.

The ship was, like *Europic Ferry*, another 1967 veteran. Then it had been the M.V. *Dragon* built for a P&O subsidiary working from Southampton.

In 1985, her owners, P&O's Normandy Ferries was sold to Townsend Thoresen, only for them in turn to be sold back to P&O in December 1986. Meanwhile Townsend Thoresen had earlier in 1986 sent the *Dragon* to Cairnryan but with a new name.

In 1958 Denny's had built the first M.V. *Ionic Ferry*, a look-alike to the *Bardic Ferry* previously seen. That *Ionic Ferry* actually opened the Cairnryan-Larne service in 1973. When *Dragon* was moved she took this auspicious name.

She was to serve the Cairnryan route from 1986 to 1992 but most of that period would be in P&O blue which makes her appearance in the Townsend Thoresen colours on the 1986 brochure noteworthy.

Inside the brochure revealed still further treasures. Quite often such publications detail further publicity literature which the collector may otherwise be un-aware of. In this case an A4 brochure for *Townsend Thoresen Holiday Coach Tours from Northern Ireland* is shown. Literature showing Townsend Thoresen-liveried coaches does exist but whether these were specifically used at Cairnryan I am not sure.

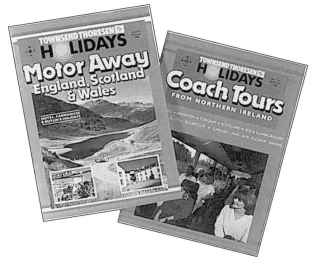

On 18 September 1988 *Ionic Ferry* was berthed at Larne wearing the P&O blue colour scheme.

Ionic Ferry's replacement in 1992 was the M.V. *Pride of Rathlin* seen here tied up at Larne on 19 May 1995.

This vessel's very distinctive outline comes straight from the Dover crossings and the series of Townsend Thoresen M.V. *Free Enterprise* ferries. This was *VII* of 1973. Along the way the name *Pride of Walmer* had also been carried but Dover had remained the port of registry as the picture shows. She worked on the North Channel for eight years until withdrawn in 2000. By then she was the last survivor with her (lineally) original owner, of the *Free Enterprise* series. She was sold for further use in Indonesia.

It is still impossible to finish with Loch Ryan. Since the 1980s two more operators have worked out of the Loch. One was very shortlived although the pedigree and tradition of the Isle of Man Steam Packet Company was otherwise impeccable.

Their traditional Scottish service has already been described at Ardrossan. Traffic there had plummeted. In 1980 20,400 passengers, two years later 9,600. Moving the service to Stranraer, which had seen the occasional Steam Packet excursion previously, would shorten the ship passage, saving time for the passengers and money for the company.

Over the 1986-1989 seasons a seasonal weekly service to Douglas was therefore offered. It was not a great success. Under 4,500 passengers were carried in 1986.

The author is unaware of separate publicity for the Stranraer sailings, reliance was placed on the main A4 company brochure. So it is a picture of the 1972 M.V. *Mona's Queen* that represents this shortlived route taken at the Stranraer Railway Pier on 7 July 1988. The coastal sailing around the Rhins of Galloway had much scenically to commend it.

The next operator had to build their own terminal at Stranraer and with them came a revolution. This was the 1992 arrival of Seacat. Seacat was a merging of Hoverspeed and Sea Containers which had brought Tasmanian, Incat-built, high speed, car carrying catamarans to the English Channel in 1990.

The 37 knot, 1991-built *Seaspeed Scotland* required a £3 million terminal to be built at Stranraer's West Pier. The service opened on 1 June 1992 and very soon the pressure on both Stena and P&O to introduce their own high-speed craft was building.

The result through the 1990s has been a superb assortment of high-speed ferry literature although by the end of the decade Seacat had removed its operation from Stranraer to Troon.

This launch brochure, on the next page, featured the record holder *Hoverspeed Great Britain* in its imagery.

It was frustrating that during the 1990s so many travel agents chose to plaster their own labels all over the attractive leaflet covers when invariably those leaflets had a space for these stickers on the back cover. It seems to show little respect for the product by these travel agents whose message seems to be to assert themselves over the actual carrier.

Some things the publicity rarely show. Bad weather off Corsewall Point is one thing. Another is the competitors' vessels. The author's photography is needed therefore to try to show some of the magic that the real vessels can engender as much as the publicity.

For sure anyone with a sense of nostalgia will always wish that they had seen a classic Denny turbine steamer like the 1931 T.S.S. *Princess Margaret*. Yet in the last years of the twentieth century amazing maritime scenes

straight out of science fiction could be witnessed off Corsewall Point.

Corsewall off which the *Princess Victoria* tragedy had developed, Corsewall whose lighthouse had so prominently featured in the best of the *Caledonian Princess* literature was now reverberating, and that is the word, to the thunder of high speed ferries.

This summer photo (above) taken on 29 August 1999 shows *Seacat Scotland* passing with the 16.15 from Stranraer. The competitive pressure was such that the Troon sailings had started and soon afterwards Stranraer was left altogether.

For the ship photographer the area provides a wealth of views. A zoom lens and a fine day enables successive shots with Ailsa Craig, the Mull of Kintye, and (in the picture) the lighthouse itself with the Antrim Coast to feature. The lighthouse had become a hotel enabling afternoon tea to feature in the excursion. The cars parked to the right of the image show how a grandstand view is possible.

By 1999 *Seacat Scotland* was small fry. The above and following pictures all date from 15 August 1998. That day three high speed ferries and four conventional ferries passed the lens around Loch Ryan. Framing the lighthouse at Corsewall are (left) P&O's 1996 *Jetliner* which is a 31 knot vessel, and Stena's (right) 1996 *Stena Voyager* which seems the ultimate in sci-fi shipping. Built in Finland this monster reaches 40 knots.

Ferries were passing each other as one arrived and one left Stranraer, following one another up and down the loch and in this picture (opposite, top), three vessels passed one another off Corsewall. The Seacat takes the inside lane at high speed whilst *Stena Galloway* (centre – once the erstwhile railway-owned *Galloway Princess*) and *Stena Caledonia* (right) were working the re-routed Stena service from Stranraer to Belfast.

That break with tradition has not proved permanent but at the time of the move prompted a landmark leaflet (previous page). The move lasted from 12 November 1995, paving the way for the HSS or High Speed Superferry's arrival, to 1 September 2000 when the conventional ferries re-opened the Larne run leading to the 2000 brochures hyping Stranraer-Larne as a new service!

Passing Cairnryan (previous page, bottom) is the *HSS Stena Voyager*. The space age design is almost overwhelming when seen close to. The lack of conventional deck space for handling warps is very evident, the crew working from the cut-outs fore and aft in the hull. Nor is there much deck space for passengers to promenade on.

Those high-speed ferries were the daily diet at Stranraer in the 1990s. What could provide a greater contrast than the view below of the harbour at Garlieston on 27 June 1992.

Some readers might wonder where Garlieston is and what little known ferry service works from there. Garlieston's crescent of houses faces east into its own bay that in turn opens into Wigtown Bay. This is Galloway's sparsely populated but fertile Machars Penninsula and the narrative has reached the Solway Firth.

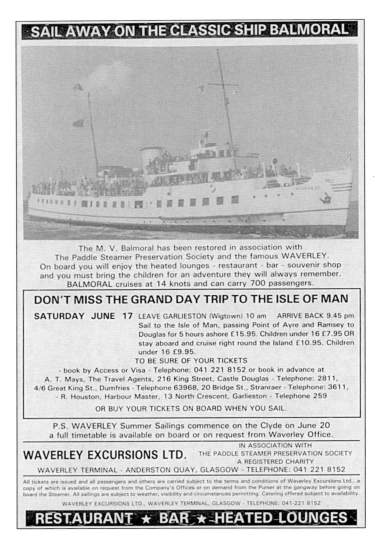

Wigtown, Garlieston, Kirkcudbright, Kippford and Carsethorn are all little-known ports on Scotland's southern coast which had once supported steamer services. Several communities along this coast retain their Steam Packet Inn. In the main these services were nineteenth century operations and well beyond the datelines of our publicity collecting,

Garlieston has proved to be a bit different. Sailings to the Isle of Man had operated from 1878 to 1953 with some gaps (McHaffie's book describes a fascinating assortment of Galloway-originating excursions).

Revival came from a strange quarter. P.S. *Waverley's* preservation owners restored in 1986 the Bristol Channel motor ship M.V. *Balmoral* and her programme has offered an annual Garlieston-Douglas excursion, the subject of the pictures on the previous page, as part of her annual perambulation of the British coast.

This has featured in their national timetable and has attracted its own leaflets like the one above for 1989.

Three

From the North Lancashire Coast

The North Lancashire Coast traditionally included the isolated area of Furness with its large port at Barrow. Linking Barrow across to Morecambe and Heysham were the activities of the Midland Railway steamships. The Midland had reached Morecambe in 1851 and a steamship service to Belfast was started. Morecambe was exposed and a service from Barrow would be less exposed so between 1891 and 1904 the service worked from there.

The use of Barrow required the services of the independent, albeit allied, Furness Railway. The result was the massive investment in creating Heysham Harbour which was opened in 1904. Since then Heysham has played an important though not consistent role in Irish Sea services.

Barrow's role in passenger shipping is now non-existent, although services had pre-dated and lasted beyond the extent of the Midland's involvement. This is why the Caledonian Railway's 1880 tourist programme (overleaf) could feature the Barrow Steam Navigation Company as part of a tourist itinerary whose railway elements encircled the Cumbrian mountains between Carlisle and Barrow by use of the LNWR and Furness systems. The Furness itself is a source of shipping publicity because before the First World War, they operated a Barrow-Fleetwood service.

It is to Heysham that the weight of interest in services from the North Lancashire coast must go.

Over the page is a glimpse of the 1930s approach to car carrying as a crane hoists a vehicle aboard the LMS-owned S.S. *Duke of Abercorn* at Heysham for the Belfast service. Are the couple at stage right the anxious owners?

Rapid inter-war traffic growth had brought the *Abercorn* to Heysham. It had been the Holyhead-Greenore *Curraghmore* of 1919 from the ubiquitous Denny yard.

The re-naming ensured harmony with the Heysham tradition of Duke names although the vessel was only at Heysham between 1928 and scrapping in 1935.

Between 1968-1970, as the Sealink brand was adopted, literature was increasingly standard-ised in design for all the BR Irish Sea routes. Prior to this the BR regional structure's influence was strong. This ensured that Fishguard and Stranraer had little commonality in presentation. Between those Western Region and Scottish Region ports lay the two London Midland Region ports of Heysham and Holyhead. There it was possible to observe a common presentation by at least the mid 1950s.

Shown on page 66 is a fine example, a parallel piece existed in the same year at Holyhead. The layout and arrowhead imagery was shared. Each route applied its own name on the entwined flower heads. A shamrock and a Lancashire rose made sense at Heysham, but why was this image used at Holyhead?

DOUGLAS (ISLE OF MAN).

CIRCULAR TOUR, Via FURNESS ABBEY and BARROW (Piel Pier).

TOURIST TICKETS,

AVAILABLE FOR TWO CALENDAR MONTHS,

(Except those issued in August and September, which will only be available up to the 30th of September,)

Are issued from the undermentioned Stations to

DOUGLAS, and vice versa,

In connection with the Barrow Steam Navigation Company's Boats:—

	1st Cl. and Saloon.		2nd Cl. and Saloon.		3rd Cl. and Steerage			1st Cl. and Saloon.		2nd Cl. and Saloon.		3rd Cl. and Steerage	
	s.	d.	s.	d.	s.	d.		s.	d.	s.	d.	s.	d.
Aberdeen,	71	11	54	0	35	10	Larbert,	44	10	33	8	22	2
Annan,	34	0	29	6	16	6	Leith,	40	0	30	0	20	0
Beattock,	40	0	30	0	20	0	Lockerbie,	40	0	30	0	20	0
Crieff,	51	11	39	0	25	10	Midcalder,	40	0	30	0	20	0
Dumfries,	36	6	30	0	18	0	Motherwell,	40	0	30	0	20	0
Dundee,	50	0	37	6	25	0	Paisley,	40	0	30	0	20	0
Edinburgh (Prin. St.),	40	0	30	0	20	0	Perth,	50	0	37	6	25	0
Forfar,	60	0	45	0	29	10	Port-Glasgow,	42	6	32	0	21	6
Glasgow (Central),	40	0	30	0	20	0	Stirling,	46	3	34	10	23	0
Greenock,	42	6	32	0	21	6	Wemyss Bay,	43	6	32	5	22	0
Hamilton.	42	0	31	8	21	3							

Passengers making the Circular Tour travel *via* Whitehaven, Furness Abbey, &c., in the going, and *via* Carnforth on the return journey, or *vice versa*. Tickets are also issued available to travel *via* Carnforth both going and returning.

Passengers are requested to state the Route by which they wish to travel when taking their Tickets.

The journey may be broken at all or any of the Stations or places on the Route, also at Kendal and Windermere.

Passengers can now travel from Scotland to Douglas in one day.

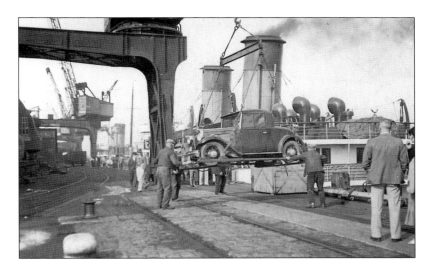

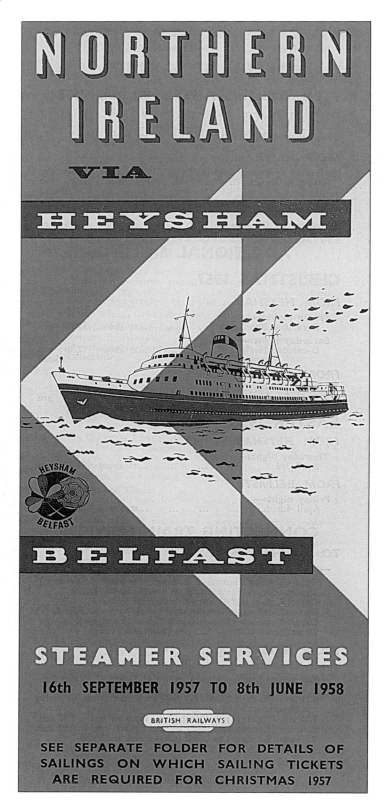

An individual ship drawing was applied and at Heysham the subject was far removed from the *Duke of Abercorn*, even if it was not yet a roll on/roll off ferry.

The subject of the drawing was also the subject of a BR London Midland Region carriage print (above). The carriage print is named, the leaflet is not, but the common theme was the advent of the three turbine powered Dukes delivered from Harland & Wolff and Denny's in 1956: Lancaster, Argyll and Rothesay.

Claude Buckle undertook the carriage print in 1957. Norman Wilcox produced a fine poster in 1956 'Three New Ships For The Heysham-Belfast Overnight Service'. An example of that sold for £1,265 at Christie's in 1999.

In the late 1960s, all three ferries were converted for roll on/roll off car carrying but when new, thoughts of car carrying were still restrained particularly in the case of what was regarded as the flagship of the three: T.S.S. *Duke of Lancaster*.

Our previous book *To Western Scottish Waters* illustrated a cruise operation run by a ferry company with Coast Lines' trips to Western Scotland from Liverpool. These steamed up the Irish Sea and through the North Channel and shortly after their demise in 1956, British Railways provided another take on the same theme.

When built the Lancaster had been outfitted for a dual role as a small cruiseship. BR cruises had started with the Southern Region's *Falaise* in 1948. The *Duke of Lancaster* joined her in 1958 and offered cruises until 1966. Most, but not all, of her cruises left from Heysham and amongst the foreign destinations like Portugal, Denmark and Belgium, the Scottish Lochs Cruise went in the wake of the Coast Line's *Killarney* tradition.

When cruising the Lancaster was transformed, one cabin even becoming a ladies' hair salon. An all volunteer crew was assembled. Memorabilia of any sort from her cruising days would be a worthy find nowadays.

1961 HOLIDAY

Cruises

by t.s.s.   "Duke of Lancaster"

CONTINENTAL CRUISES

12-day cruises in May and June
visiting Norway, Denmark and Holland

6-day cruise in June
visiting Holland and Belgium

SCOTTISH LOCHS CRUISES

10-day Spring and Autumn Cruises
visiting the lovely West Coast of Scotland

LONDON MIDLAND

Enjoy a Rail/Sea Cruise

Every Tuesday from 10 July to 14 August 1973 a Sealink vessel S.S. 'Duke of Lancaster' or S.S. 'Duke of Argyll' will sail from Heysham at 11.00 for a cruise in the Solway Firth area returning at 18.00

Catering
A restaurant, cafeteria, tea bar and two licensed bars (with bar snacks available) will be open throughout the cruise.

Entertainment
Entertainment will be provided during the cruise — bingo, discotheque and group etc. These will be so organised as not to spoil the enjoyment of passengers not taking part.

Please see overleaf for details of special inclusive Rail/Cruise fare and train times.

 **British Rail**

Amongst these little known gems must be a flimsy two-sided leaflet I found marking a final stab at cruising. For six Tuesdays in the high summer of 1973, the Lancaster or the Argyll offered a seven-hour Solway Firth cruise out of Heysham. A special connecting train was even laid on from Nelson and the East Lancashire line.

The three ships saw the end of the Heysham–Belfast route in 1975. The Rothesay was scrapped that year. The Argyll actually closed the service and was then sold for further service from Greece. The *Duke of Lancaster* survived with Sealink until 1979 before she was sold for use as a static hotel ship at Mostyn on the North Wales Coast. This was not successful and when photographed on 28 November 1992 (opposite, top), the ship, whilst still in relatively good condition, was bereft of much activity.

Postcard coverage of passenger shipping is always intense. An extra cachet applies to postcards issued officially by a vessel's operators. These have been thoroughly catalogued in the case of railway owned shipping. The work of Alsop (see bibliography) and of the Railway Postcard Collectors Circle is recommended.

In other chapters, a 1911 official from the Larne–Stranraer route is shown and some analysis of the LNWR officials associated with the Holyhead route will be given. Here, some notes on the Heysham cards are provided as an indicator of the scope of the subject. Three operators from Heysham are involved: the Midland Railway, the LMS and British Railways.

Around 1904, the Midland issued eight cards in connection with the new services from Heysham. Subsequently at least a further thirty cards from that company and associated with that route have been traced by Alsop.

After the 1923 grouping, the mantle fell on the LMS who were investing in new ships. They produced at least eight cards.

British Railways and Sealink continued the tradition. Cards for the three 1956 Heysham Dukes in their original black hull/ buff funnel and later Sealink rail blue finish all exist. The example shown is of the rail blue *Rothesay*. A similar card seen for the *Argyll* does provide a slightly different angle – the cards were individual for the three sisters.

Amongst the BR Sealink card series, other Irish Sea favourites like the *Caledonian Princess*, *Antrim Princess* and the soon to be discussed *Manx Viking* feature.

NORTHERN IRELAND
Sea Link
CONTAINER
SERVICE

BRITISH RAILWAYS

BR's publicity enables a swift change of focus from postcards to freight to take place. Freight publicity is always going to be harder to obtain than that for passenger operations. A reasonable amount does survive from BR's Irish Sea operations so either I have been unusually fortunate or else the nature of British Railways allowed better publicity to be produced and wider distribution to be achieved. Additionally through the 1950s and 1960s, BR underwent two revolutions in swift succession in the name of containerisation, which they were determined to publicise. Examples from Heysham and Holyhead will be seen.

The first is from Heysham where in October 1958, BR inaugurated their first dedicated unit-load shipping service. Two new vessels, called the M.V. *Container Enterprise* and M.V. *Container Venturer*, were used. The former is on this leaflet's cover. Around 1958-1959 and following the 1954 lead in the Irish Sea by the Anglo-Continental Container Service out of Preston, BR was introducing the technology to dedicated ships widely.

As hindsight showed, this was with the wrong sort of container. The containers employed could trace their ancestry on the railway back to the 1920s. In the Irish trade, they had obvious potential carrying foodstuffs.

One result was this 1958 leaflet for the new service. Another noteworthy element was the adoption of the 'Sealink' word. Was this its first use by British Railways?

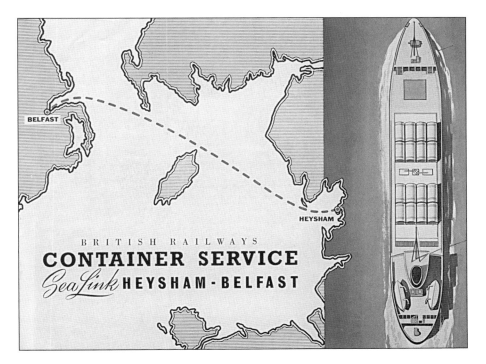

Inside, the Sealink theme continued and the overhead view of the ship showed the serried ranks of containers. They resemble tanks because of their curved roofs which was where the problem lay. The leaflet showed a container with its door open on a typical meat cargo but these boxes did not stack up.

Virtually overnight in 1965, the International Standards Organisation or I.S.O. box made its mark. Engineered to different dimensions, international in concept and stackable, it made BR's 1950s investment (which went well beyond the Irish Sea) redundant. A new word entered the vocabulary: Freightliner. Later in their lives, the two ships were adapted to carry the I.S.O. containers.

The period between 1968 and 1970 witnessed the development of the standardised marketing that produced the Sealink brand. The changes took those couple of years to come about.

Looking at 1968, the result was literature still produced by the London Midland Region, like this leaflet, but with a cover used more widely. The author is not sure how effective 'Stran, Hey, Holy, Fish' was, even if the 'British Rail Irish Seaways' header was clear enough.

This cover is known to the author for the Holyhead route that season. It was also used on a twelve-page brochure with the catchy slogan inside 'Go STRANHEYHOLYFISH!' That was for 1968 as a whole which suggests that these covers were used for all that year's issues. However I still await examples from Fishguard and Stranraer until which time one wonders if their local management avoided being corralled into what was not the best marketing initiative?

In 1970 covers very similiar to the one below made their appearance on all the Irish Sea routes. Sealink was established. The core image was changed in 1972 from a map to an image of train and ship. With variations the latter continued to 1980.

Hence there is a run of similar material available in numerous editions and not so difficult to find throughout the 1970s. One blatant exception is illustrated here.

The design is standard, the route is anything but. The *Princess Victoria* tragedy claimed 134 lives in 1953, the Britannia Bridge fire of 23 May 1970 did not kill anyone but caused considerably more disruption. For twenty months until January 1972, there was no rail link to Holyhead. More will be revealed in the Holyhead chapter, but one consequence of the emergency was the transfer of some freight and all the mail services – not the car ferry – to Heysham.

It is easy to assume that this is a timetable for this re-located operation between Heysham-Dublin Dun Laoghaire. The ships used were the Holyhead mail route twins M.V. *Cambria* and *Hibernia* and the service ceased on 30 January 1972.

The author was surprised to discover that this was not the case. The overnight mail boat operation from Heysham was covered by timetables which continued to be headed Holyhead and which will be seen in that chapter.

However, and it is easy for this to confuse commentators, BR had in any event planned a summer only car ferry service between Heysham and Dun Laoghaire to start from 27 June 1970. The timetable illustrated, with its daylight sailings and references to the use of the M.V. *Dover* and *Holyhead Ferry 1,* is for this operation.

In terms of the timetables, the proof of this is contained in the first Sealink annual timeable, an A4 brochure issued late in 1969 that featured the route as a new service. Mint copies of this keynote document should contain a letter which refers to the new Sealink name and this new service.

In summary, the car ferry was planned and public knowledge by early 1970, however it was timetabled to start after the then unplanned movement of the mail boats from Holyhead.

This car ferry route was aimed at passengers from Northern England. There was even a special connecting train to Heysham Harbour from Leeds for it.

The new route was not a success and did not operate after 1971. This means there should only be two timetable leaflets for it, of which this would be the second.

When the Heysham–Belfast passenger sailings by BR ceased in 1975 some of the crews managed to transfer to a joint BR/Belfast Steamship Company freight service that had been started up. Ships like the M.V. *Penda*, later to be the Isle of Man Steam Packet's M.V. *Peveril* were involved.

The Isle of Man was to influence matters at Heysham greatly in succeeding years. When the Midland Railway opened Heysham in 1904, they had started a service to Douglas. The Isle of Man Steam Packet took this over in 1927. After the Second World War, the service was very limited. The company gave it up in 1974 which provides the interest in this brochure for its final season. It had been worked by the classic turbine packet steamers, like T.S.S. *Manxman,* throughout.

The Isle of Man Steam Packet Co. Ltd.
(Incorporated in the Isle of Man)

EXCURSIONS BY SEA

Summer Season — 1974

HAPPY HOLIDAYS

BY SEA

to

ISLE OF MAN

Day Excursions — Party Outings
School Educational Parties

between

FLEETWOOD & DOUGLAS

and

HEYSHAM & DOUGLAS

With Sealink's Belfast service about to be withdrawn too, the Isle of Man Steam Packet hardly thought that Heysham might again provide it with serious competition.

In 1978 that assumption was proved terribly wrong. On the island there was great frustration that a roll on/roll off service had not been provided by the Steam Packet. Road hauliers felt especially inconvenienced.

With Manx government interest, a roll on/roll off linkspan was built at Douglas in 1977 – without a ship to use it. That changed when a 1976 Spanish ferry became the M.V. *Manx Viking* of the new Manx Line company. The Bamforth's postcard shows her in all her early glory with Manx Line funnel colours.

The service did not have an easy ride at first. Everyone wanted it, bar the Steam Packet, but there were breakdowns and some dreadful weather wrecked the Douglas linkspan too.

Originally very much a Manx operation, in November 1978, James Fisher of Barrow and Sealink/BR took over. Sealink extended their interest over the next two years and the result was Sealink Manx Line. The route then prospered and provided the Steam Packet with serious competition.

Pure Manx Line literature will be very hard to find (the author had none until the day before this book went to the publisher!). Due to the process of privatisation and merger, Sealink Manx Line is only a bit more common, though in total, a small file's worth was probably issued.

The example (opposite top) came from the managerial hand of a Mr Martin Miller to whom credit was given for ensuring that 'it eventually became impossible to set foot inside one of Britain's motorway service, coach or railway stations without being confonted by one of the colourful and effective posters produced by Sealink Isle of Man'.

The Sealink Isle of Man brand is clear on this leaflet which offered tempting day excursions, one of which promised a free Douglas horse tram ticket. The artwork for the ship was simple but recognisable. A little detail of note was the Manx Line funnel colour arrangement which was reproduced in the artwork – compare with the postcard. The vessel in full Manx Line colours had had two pages to its route in the 1980 Sealink annual brochure, the sort of exposure that the new service needed.

The BR-issued Sealink Manx Line material is likely to cover the 1980-1984 seasons. Privatisation came in 1984. However next year, the seven year rollercoaster of the M.V. *Manx Viking's* Manx service climaxed when Sea Containers who then owned Sealink, did a deal with the Steam Packet and merged the operations. *Manx Viking* did get Steam Packet colours ex-Sealink blue but left the service in September 1986. The Manx Line company was itself not wound up by Sea Containers until 2000. When Sealink had been sold by Sea Containers to Stena, Sea Containers had retained their interest in the Steam Packet operation in which, since 1996, a controlling interest has been owned.

This little item below is a small timetable card in a generic style Sealink applied across their routes in 1984. Each route had its own vessel drawn into the porthole view and by now *Manx Viking* had Sealink on her hull.

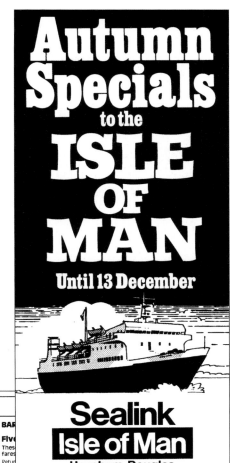

Autumn Specials to the ISLE OF MAN

Until 13 December

Sealink Isle of Man
Heysham–Douglas

Sealink Isle of Man
Heysham – Douglas

SCHEDULES & FARES 1984
For more information about Sealink Isle of Man please contact:-
Sealink, Sea Terminal, Heysham, Lancs, LA3 2XF.
Telephone: 0524 53802
or:
Sealink, Sea Terminal, Douglas, Isle of Man
Telephone: 0624 24241
For your copy of the Sealink Isle of Man 1984 brochure,
Dial-a-Brochure on Preston (0772) 24221 ....Anytime!

FARES

Passengers	Single	Return
Adult passengers	£18.00	£36.00
Children 5 and under 16	£9.00	£18.00
Children under 5	Free	Free
Holders of Young Persons & Senior Citizens Railcards	£9.00	£18.00
Dogs conveyed in owner's car	Free	Free
Guide Dogs	Free	Free

Accompanied Vehicles	Single	Return
Cars, Motor Caravans & Caravanettes	£40.00	£80.00
Motorcycles	£15.50	£31.00

BAR

Five
Thes
fares
Retur
the fi
have
arriva

9 January to 30 March and 1 October to 24 December.
Adult Passengers £25
Cars £50
Motorcycles £25
31 March to 30 September
Adult passengers £30
Cars £60
Motorcycles £30
Children 5 and under 16 half price.
Not available on 1415 Heysham-Douglas and 0830 Douglas-Heysham services on Saturdays 26 May to 15 September.

1984 SAILING SCHEDULE

Heysham → Douglas Crossing time about 3¾ hours (2355 departure is scheduled to arrive at 0700) Car check-in time 45 minutes before departure.

Douglas → Heysham Crossing time about 3¾ hours Car check-in time 45 minutes before departure.

Heysham → Douglas

9 January to 24 December
(No service 1 to 8 January and 25 to 31 December)

Time	Days of operation from the Mainland
1415	Mondays to Saturdays until 28 April and from 29 October Daily 29 April to 28 October
2355	Daily 24 May to 23 September

Douglas → Heysham

9 January to 24 December
(No service 1 to 8 January and 25 to 31 December)

Time	Days of operation from the island
0830	Mondays to Saturdays until 28 April and from 29 October Daily 29 April to 28 October
1915	Daily 24 May to 23 September

Manx Line Ltd accepts no liability for any inaccuracy in this information which may be altered at any time, prices and timings are subject to alteration without notice.

Sealink Isle of Man
Heysham – Douglas

A number of A4 brochures for the Sealink Isle of Man service exist. The cover of 1984's with the Laxey Wheel was unambiguous. This was the last railway issue.

Inside there were five views of the ship in colour showing the rail blue hull, Sealink slogan, and red funnels with Manx three-legged symbol (called a triskelion). She never carried BR double arrows. Nor did she gain the white hull and colours of Sealink British Ferries despite the privatised 1985 Sealink Isle of Man brochure. which was the last in the series, having a whole series of artwork views of her in those colours.

One of the 1984 views is reproduced and shows *Manx Viking* at the Douglas linkspan. All sorts of peripherals could be followed up by the collector and this double page spread leads into some of them. The service benefitted by being part of the national network as the map shows and so through tickets could be sought but...

Heysham Harbour station had closed with the Belfast service in 1975. Eventually, in 1987, after the Steam Packet had returned to Heysham and left Liverpool, it would re-open but, for the duration of the *Manx Viking's* service, a bus connection from Lancaster station was offered. One of the inset images shows a Lancaster City Transport Leyland Leopard with the then unusual (for England) Alexander of Falkirk Y type body in dedicated Sealink Isle of Man livery.

A list of public service vehicles that have carried Sealink livery would be surprisingly extensive (one has already been seen earlier) and it even includes a horse tram. Page twelve of this brochure carried a generously-sized image of Douglas Corporation Number 1 in Sealink livery on the Promenade. There can be no doubt that *Manx Viking* and her operators had made quite a splash on the Island scene.

On the Fylde Penninsula of the Lancashire Coast lies the port of Fleetwood. Once again it was largely the creation of railway money, in this case the Lancashire & Yorkshire with the London & North Western Railways, thanks to whom an Irish service operated until the economies of the LMS closed it in 1928 in favour of Heysham. Fleetwood, like Silloth, is nowadays run by Associated British Ports by which means it preserves its railway ancestry.

Fleetwood retained its Manx services but roll on/roll off was a long time coming. Instead, for six years from 1940-1946 Fleetwood was the sole mainland port for the island. Post-war Fleetwood hosted a seasonal I.O.M.S.P.Co service using their traditional vessels.

This was run until a first closure in 1961. Sailings were resumed in 1971 until 5 September 1985 when, as a consequence of the merger with Sea Containers and Manx Line leading to the concentration of services at Heysham, Fleetwood was abandoned again. Not for too long however. Thanks to Associated British Ports' interest, excursions were restored in 1986, since when quite a variety of limited Manx operations have been offered, even extending to a Fleetwood-Dublin service worked by the Steam Packet.

Our choice from what could be a wealth of purely Manx-Fleetwood material services the thought that a very considerable amount of Manx shipping literature was issued through the mainland railway operators.

Without doubt the busiest period for the Manx services is at TT time in May/June. Motor cycle racing takes place again in September for the Manx Grand Prix. It is to that event that this British Railways handbill refers in offering an excursion from the Fylde communities to Douglas. Who today would think of taking a train from St Annes at 10.53 p.m., changing at Kirkham and Wesham, continuing on their short journey up the Fylde Penninsula to Fleetwood and then so it looks, waiting for about $2\frac{1}{2}$ hours for a departure at 2.30 a.m.? A guaranteed long day out with no hint as to a return arrival time.

PLEASE RETAIN THIS BILL FOR REFERENCE

MANX GRAND PRIX MOTOR CYCLE RACES
Tuesday & Thursday 6th & 8th September

DAY EXCURSION TICKETS
TO
DOUGLAS
ISLE OF MAN
Via Fleetwood and Isle of Man Steam Packet Co. Ltd.

MONDAY & WEDNESDAY NIGHTS 5th & 7th SEPTEMBER

FROM	Times of Departure	RETURN FARES		
		First Class Throughout	3rd Class Rail and 1st Class Steamer	3rd Class Throughout
	p.m.	s d	s d	s d
PRESTON	11 8	24 / 5	22 /11	18 /11
ST. ANNES ON SEA	10A 53	26 / 9	24 / 6	20 / 6
ANSDELL & FAIRHAVEN ...	10A 57	26 / 6	24 / 3	20 / 3
LYTHAM ...	11A 2	26 / –	24 / –	20 / –
KIRKHAM & WESHAM ...	11 30	22 /11	21 /11	17 /11
BLACKPOOL North	11 15	22 / 3	21 / 6	17 / 6
LAYTON	11 18	21 /11	21 / 3	17 / 3
POULTON	11 43	21 / 9	21 / 2	17 / 2
THORNTON CLEVELEYS ...	11 46	21 / 5	20 /11	16 /11
FLEETWOOD Steamer depart	2 30 am			
DOUGLAS arrive approx.	6 0 am			
A—Change at Kirkham & W.				

RETURN ARRANGEMENTS
Passengers return from DOUGLAS at 4.0 pm or 6.0 pm

Children under three years of age, free; three years and under fourteen, half-fares
Conditions of issue of Excursion and Other Tickets at less than Ordinary Fare
These Tickets are issued subject to the British Transport Commission's published Regulations and Conditions applicable to British Railways exhibited at their Stations or obtainable free of charge at Station Booking Offices.
Tickets can be obtained in advance at BLACKPOOL (NORTH AND CENTRAL) STATIONS also from the following agencies:-
CO-OPERATIVE SOCIETY LTD., New Central Buildings, Coronation Street, Blackpool, E. & A. TRAVEL AGENCY, Metropole Buildings, Blackpool. Messrs. FRAME'S TOURS LTD., 18 Abingdon Street, Blackpool. STANLEY LORDS' AGENCY, Victoria Square, Cleveleys. Messrs. PICKFORDS LTD., 63 Bolton Street, Blackpool. Messrs. THOS COOK & SON LTD., C/o. R.H.O. HILLS, Blackpool Ltd., Bank Hey Street, Blackpool. E. HADLEY, Marton Post Office, 6 Preston New Rd.
Further information will be supplied on application to Stations, Official Railway Agents, or to Mr. T. W. Polding, District Passenger Manager, (London Midland Region), Hunts Bank, Manchester, 3. Telephone No. BLA 3456. Extension 566.

July, 1955   XA/I.O.M.   B.R. 35000

BRITISH RAILWAYS

Hills Printers, Chorley   E652

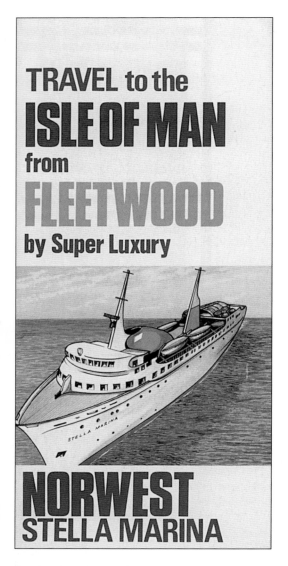

TRAVEL to the
ISLE OF MAN
from
FLEETWOOD
by Super Luxury

NORWEST
STELLA MARINA

By this point of the voyage it ought to be clear, that whilst the core group of operators in various incarnations provide continuity, there have been a good number, even in recent times, of what the bus operator would call the 'independent'. Finding their publicity is always a challenge, and there is much that the author misses. Around the item shown however, a good tale can be told.

From the previous caption it will be noted that there was a decade between 1961-1971 when Fleetwood was entirely deserted by the I.O.M.S.P. Co.

Norwest Hovercraft Limited (the name is tucked away on the leaflet's back cover) had been created to open a hovercraft service to the Island. That never happened but for the 1969 season they chartered the M.V. *Stella Marina* to operate the Fleetwood route with some success.

The cover's rendition was quite comic-strip as was some of the interior artwork but an interior monochrome (below) confirmed that she was real enough. She went back to her Norwegian owners at the end of the season and the solution for 1970 took a step back in time. Norwest obtained the erstwhile MacBraynes' vessel M.V. *Locheil* as their *Norwest Laird*. She was not a patch on her predecessor lacking the comforts and being slow. The service petered out that year and it was the Steam Packet who revived it the next year.

When roll on/roll off did arrive at Fleetwood it was thanks to an investment by the then owners, the nationalised British Transport Docks Board who in 1974 opened a tidal roll on/roll off berth.

Almost overnight Fleetwood knocked Preston out of the story. P&O decided to move in with two brand new lorry ferries, the M.V. *Bison* and the *Buffalo*.

Thereafter the story has been one of sheer success. Ferrymasters was incorporated into the operation and the Pandoro (for P&O Roll on/Roll off) brand adopted. Here on 16 August 1986, *Buffalo* leaves Fleetwood for Belfast. In 1998 she became the *European Leader* on their Liverpool–Dublin service.

As usual, freight publicity is not so easy to find, contacts with trucking company offices are needed. This rather nice celebration of Pandoro's twenty-first birthday was found in 1996. At the time the Fleetwood to Larne services were still being worked by *Buffalo* and *Bison*. The M.V. *Ibex* is featured on the cover. It had been built for the Pandoro Irish Sea Services in 1979, but was chartered out to North Sea Ferries between 1980–1995 only to re-appear as the *Ibex* again in the Irish Sea in 1995. The Pandoro brand was replaced in 1997 by the P&O European Ferries (Irish Sea) label but the headquarters remained at Fleetwood. At this time the Irish Sea freight operations and the Cairnryan passenger ferries were merged administratively.

Are you going to

NORTHERN IRELAND?

(with or without your car)

then *GO*

T.F.S.

TRANSPORT FERRY SERVICE

the COMFORT way!

Effective 1st January 1969, cancelling all previous issues.

At the base of the Fylde, Preston Docks had opened in 1882 and closed in 1981. A factor in their demise was the difficulty of accommodating larger ships and the necessity to dredge the Ribble since the port was 22km from the open sea.

The Docks were municipally controlled and this had helped welcome new entrants to the scene. In particular in the post-war years both the Atlantic Steam Navigation Company's Transport Ferry Service and the Anglo-Continental Container Service were established there.

A.S.N., although a pre-war company, had really come to prominence thanks to Captain Frank Bustard and his purchase of former tank landing craft which he turned into vehicle ferries. The Preston-Larne route opened in 1948. Nationalisation took place in 1954 but the concern went under British Transport Commission and not British Railways control.

New ships appeared from 1957 with the Denny built *Bardic Ferry* at Preston followed by *Ionic Ferry* – illustrated in our coverage of Cairnryan.

In 1969, it was said that such was their success that the ' "Transport Ferry Service" has become a by-word in the world of international trade.'

Praise indeed, but in 1971, they were privatised becoming part of the European Ferries Group. T.F.S. is hardly a household name today, yet when this leaflet was issued in 1969, they ran services from Preston to all of Larne, Belfast, Drogheda and Dublin.

Preston was finally left in 1974 consequent upon the company finding more success with their Cairnryan operation. By then another company had been and gone from Preston. This was the Felixstowe-based Ferrymasters. They started out of Preston in 1972 but swiftly moved to Fleetwood in June 1973.

The T.F.S. ships were the future as far as cargo handling on the Irish Sea went and much of the innovation took place at Preston. Preston also provided a home for other freight ferry operators. In the appendix, a list of the unit load and lorry ferry operators working in the Irish Sea in 1971 and 1998 is provided which reveals the pace of change. It is a picture of such depth and complexity that this volume can be no more than a sketch.

Four

Liverpool and the Manx Connection

Little nineteenth-century publicity will survive and much that does will be with institutions. Oddly enough one sort of institution has proved to be a source for my own collecting. The nineteenth century saw many religious houses founded or re-founded. A century and a half later, many were closing down. Their libraries tended to discard little and in the last years of the twentieth century, I was surprised by what could come to light.

This route supplied what must be one of the earliest railway guides *Freeling's London Birmingham Liverpool Manchester Railway Companion*. It appeared in various editions. From that of 1838, four pages are reproduced (to their actual and small size) advertising the Irish Sea services then operational from Liverpool.

Liverpool has for centuries been a great international port in which the Irish traffic has, like that of Glasgow, co-existed with many other trades. In another parallel, the links by immigration into the local community, add an edge.

THE

ST. GEORGE STEAM PACKET

COMPANY'S

POWERFUL STEAM SHIPS

SAIL REGULARLY, WITH OR WITHOUT PILOTS, AND **WITH** LIBERTY TO TOW SHIPS, AS UNDER:—

FROM LIVERPOOL,

For BEAUMARIS, BANGOR, AND MENAI BRIDGE, Every *Tuesday, Thursday,* and *Saturday* Morning during Summer, at Half-past Nine o'Clock, from George's Pier Head, with Passengers only.

For CORK—Every *Saturday* Evening.

For DUNDALK—Every *Wednesday* Morning.

For NEWRY—Every *Monday* and *Thursday* Evening.

FROM LONDON,

For BOSTON—Every *Tuesday* Morning.

For EXETER—(Calling at Deal, Ryde, and Cowes) weather permitting, every *Wednesday* Morning.

For PORTSMOUTH, PLYMOUTH, FALMOUTH, AND CORK— Every *Saturday* Morning.

For STOCKTON—(Calling off Scarborough and Whitby) weather permitting, every *Saturday* Evening.

FROM HULL.

For HAMBURGH—Every *Tuesday, Thursday,* and *Saturday.*

For ROTTERDAM—Every *Wednesday.*

For LEITH—Every *Wednesday.*

FROM BRISTOL.

For CORK—Every *Tuesday* and *Saturday.*

For DUBLIN—Every *Tuesday* and *Saturday.*

FROM DUBLIN.

For CORK—Every Five Days.

For GLASGOW—Every Five Days.

For BRISTOL—Every *Tuesday* and *Friday.*

FROM LUBECK TO YSTAD AND STOCKHOLM.

Every *Tuesday* during Summer.

THE COMPANY'S OFFICES

ARE

AT WATER STREET AND CLARENCE DOCK, LIVERPOOL;

137, LEADENHALL STREET, LONDON;

MINERVA TERRACE, HULL;

11, EDEN QUAY, DUBLIN;

AND AT ALL THE ABOVE PORTS.

In 1838, the three key players are seen as The St George Steam Packet Company, The City of Dublin Steam Packet Company, and The Glasgow and Liverpool Steam Shipping Company.

It is immediately obvious that traffic to other mainland British ports was as important as the Irish trade at the time. Services along the North Wales Coast will be encountered again in this chapter. The railways were then in their infancy and the direct London to Glasgow journey of 1838 involved a long sail through the Irish Sea and up the Firth of Clyde. The early appearance of J.&G. Burns of Glasgow is significant, although they had even then been in shipping for thirteen years.

The St George's Steam Packet company with a list of operations around Britain appears like an ancestor of Coast Lines – which is exactly what it was. Established in Liverpool in 1821, its lineage ran into the City of Cork Steam Packet company, whose 1950s publicity appears later and thence into B&I.

The City of Dublin Steam Packet went the same way – into B&I. That however did not take place until after the First World War. Prior to that, the company had become the dominant concern in the Dublin trade holding the prestigious Dun Laoghaire (or Kingstown as then named) to Holyhead mail contact whilst also sailing twice a day between Dublin and Liverpool. The loss of the mail contract and the disturbed Irish situation proved its downfall.

To generations of holidaymakers intent on escaping the cares of mainland Britain, Liverpool was the port *par excellence* for the Manx traffic which must form a second key strand in this chapter.

The Isle of Man Steam Packet had been serving Liverpool since 1830 and most of our focus is on the post-Second World War publicity. Whilst scene setting, a glimpse can be had of one of the fleet's significant earlier members.

P.S. *Mona's Queen* is seen in the Mersey off Cammell Laird's Birkenhead yards. Built at Barrow in 1885, she served the company until 1929 apart from First World War service as a troop ship. After that war, it was Cammell Laird who refitted her.

Ardrossan Harbour (or once the twin stations of Montgomerie and Winton Piers), Stranraer Harbour, Larne Harbour, Heysham Harbour, Dun Laoghaire Pier, Fishguard and Rosslare Harbours, all these were the names of dedicated maritime stations for the Irish traffic. Amongst the most complex to operate was Liverpool Riverside.

Glasgow, the other comparable port in this account did not have a dedicated port station within the city. At both Glasgow and Liverpool, port operations were independent of the railway, thus Liverpool Riverside Station was the property of the Mersey Docks & Harbour Board.

Strictly speaking the Irish Sea ferry services did not have much call on Riverside whose prime purpose was servicing the transatlantic liners. The Belfast Shipping Company vessels used the adjacent Princes Dock and famously their T.S.S. *Ulster Duke* collided with the railway swing bridge leading to the station on 21 October 1949 closing it for six months.

Riverside had opened in 1895 and when the last train left on 25 February 1971, it was a ten coach troop train returning soldiers from the conflict in Ulster. The image below probably reflects the scene in the second decade of the station's life when the Webb 0-6-0ST engines of the LNWR handled much of the traffic.

Riverside Railway Station. LIVERPOOL.

The Manxman

Restaurant Car Express

LONDON (Euston) and LIVERPOOL (Lime Street)

WEEKDAYS

	am		pm
London (Euston) .... dep	10 30	Liverpool (Lime Street) .... dep	2† 0
	pm	Rugby (Midland) .. .. .. arr	4 9
Liverpool (Lime Street) .. .. arr	2*15	London (Euston) .... „	5 45

* A connecting steamer for Douglas, Isle of Man, leaves Liverpool (Landing Stage) at 3.30 pm, (except Tuesday, September 18th to Friday, September 21st inclusive).
† Passengers from the Isle of Man by Isle of Man Steam Packet Co.'s steamer leave Douglas 9.0 am.

Despite the general lack of trains to Riverside for Manx traffic, there was no shortage of dedicated Manx literature issued by British Railways.

One item can prompt considerable comment. Simply speaking, what is adjacent is the cover of a leaflet about the Isle of Man as a holiday venue published by BR in 1958.

It is an attractive twelve-sided folder illustrated in monochrome and with a considerable amount of artwork in addition to the cover which is signed Daphne Padden.

The item is in series in three ways, each of which, could inspire a collection. It is one from upwards of forty 'territorial' folder titles. BR seems to have published these as early as 1949. In general they died out around 1963-1964. The Manx one continued until 1979.

The author knows of eleven different cover designs for this title, several of which were re-used in different years. These varying annual editions add another layer of interest as does the signed artwork. Work from Ellis Silas, Daphne Padden, D. Lore and Ronald Maddox is associated with this title.

Daphne Padden's signature could lead into a collection of her own pieces. Her work appeared on different BR items from at least 1956 to 1976. Their common thread appears to be London Midland Region issue.

The reverse of the leaflet holds out some interesting travel opportunities. One route involved flying from Blackpool Squires Gate aerodrome with Silver City Airways and individual handbills for this certainly exist (issued by at least the airline, BR and also the Ribble bus company).

There was a dedicated boat train called *The Manxman* which for years ran from Euston to Lime Street Station. The boat train should have its own LMR named train leaflet (an *Irish Mail* example comes later). It regularly appeared with an entry to itself in the summary of named trains at the front of each issue of the London Midland Region timetable, the entry from the summer of 1951 is shown. From those pages of named trains the *The Irish Mail,* and *The Ulster Express* (Via Heysham) also featured Irish Sea services. A further named train introduced by the LMR was *The Emerald Isle Express* (to Holyhead) and the Scottish Region had traditionally co-operated *The Northern Irishman* (to Stranraer). BR additionally

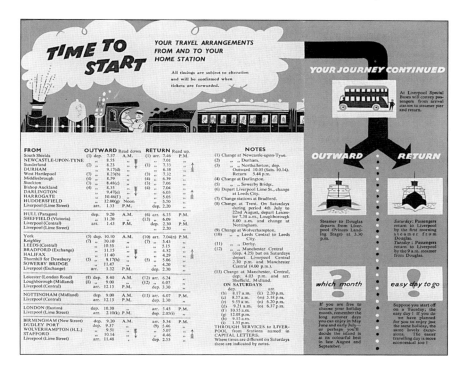

introduced *The Shamrock* in the mid 1950s, which was a service from London to Liverpool Lime Street to connect with the night boats to Dublin and Belfast. It was not particularly long lived as a namer.

At the turn of the millennium the collector would be quite likely to pick up an Isle of Man Magic Holiday brochure cover. Forty years before and the buzz was with the unpronounceable CTAC, seen as illustration 8 of the colour section. The initials stood for the Creative Tourist Agents' Conference.

Over a number of years a range of such brochures appeared – an Irish-themed one comes later. The innovation was that these were complete package holidays using the train via Liverpool. Cheaper versions of the leaflet selling the same product but from specific groups of local stations appeared as BR handbills.

Inside (above) few concessions to modernity were made in the depiction of train and coaches although an adjacent monochrome of the *Manxman* steamer of 1955 was fairly up to date. The timetables hint at the areas served. Notwithstanding baggage-laden holiday-makers, the passengers who arrived at any of Central, Lime Street or Exchange had then to resort to a bus link. As the years passed the public came to expect something more sophisticated but nothing radical happened to the Manx services until the *Manx Viking* came along.

Amongst the most extravagant of the give-aways in the 1950s, in material issued by the Steam Packet itself, was the fifty page 1958 summer services brochure (illustration 9 of the colour section).

The cover vessel is un-named but stands for one of six similar Cammell Laird vessels commencing with T.S.S. *King Orry* in 1945 and ending in the *Manxman* of 1955. The artwork is signed but is undecipherable.

Inside the brochure was packed with information. Apart from the full timetable of sailings this included two pages about the fleet, summary Manx railway timetables, adverts for the

CTAC holidays, details of the day excursions to and from the island etc. One of these was the Heysham excursion referred to earlier yet which this brochure's map failed to show.

T.S.S. *Manxman* had her own named monochrome within the 1958 brochure, an image that was considerably re-used, for instance on the cover of an offprint folder which reproduced the timetable pages alone from the main booklet. She came to be seen as the fleet's flagship and carried out a very varied programme, even on 16 July 1956 running an excursion from Belfast to Rothesay, and in 1961 spending five days on the Burns & Laird Ardrossan-Belfast service. Latterly her fame came from being the last essentially passenger, British-flagged, steam turbine packet not just in the Manx fleet but operating anywhere in Britain.

Books were written just about her and then she became a filmstar. In character she owed even more to the 1930s than the 1950s. In 1980 she assumed the identity of the Cunarder *Carpathia* in a *Titanic* film. Her most famous role was probably in *Chariots of Fire* of 1982 with Birkenhead's antiquated Woodside Pier doubling as Dover.

It was a high note to leave on. 1982 was *Manxman's* final season. She was quite simply a lovely antique with no relevance to the future of Manx services and arguably the Steam Packet's refusal to modernise had led to the whole *Manx Viking* affair and ultimately the Sea Containers take-over.

From the many ports *Manxman* was associated with, a scene of her at Liverpool Landing Stage on the evening of 20 June 1982 offers a view of her Indian Summer. There was then less than three months to go before the 'Finished with Engines' charter on 4 September.

Actually her engines had not turned their last, though they soon did. There was one more film charter and then a final sail to Preston Docks on 1 October 1982.

Manxman's prestige had secured for her an after life. It is one that has gone on for years though in sadder and sadder circumstances. Initially as a leisure ship in Preston Docks, she retained her classic black/red colours. On 31 December 1984, she was still a relatively fine sight.

She was later towed, via a stay in Liverpool, to the east coast of Britain becoming a restaurant ship at Hull and losing her Manx colours. Then there was a fire on board and, in 1997, she wound up on the Wear at Pallion Engineering, Sunderland, where despite some hopes of renovation, she continued to deteriorate into the new millennium.

Emotion makes it difficult to ignore the *Manxman* but the Steam Packet really needed to address the business of roll on/roll off much earlier than it did. There are pictures showing cars stuffed along the gangways and decks of *Manxman*.

This requirement was tackled in 1962 with the T.S.S. *Manx Maid* capable of carrying seventy cars. She was followed in 1966 by the T.S.S. *Ben-my-Chree*. At first *Manx Maid* had had her own individual brochure, shown is that of 1963. By 1967 the car ferry brochure featured both ships on its cover.

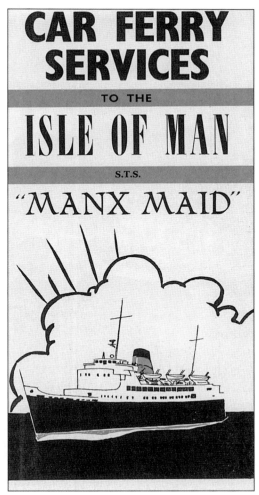

CAR FERRY SERVICES

TO THE

ISLE OF MAN

S.T.S.

"MANX MAID"

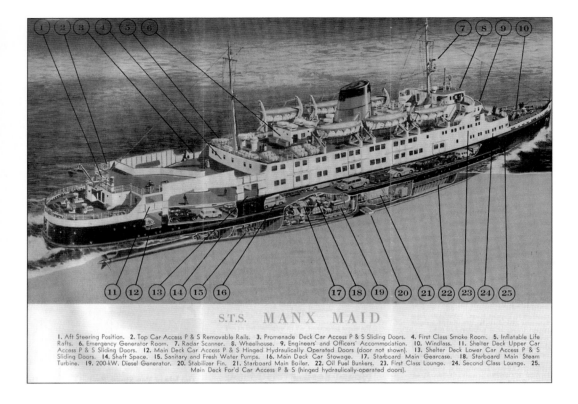

S.T.S. MANX MAID

I. Aft Steering Position. 2. Top Car Access P & S Removable Rails. 3. Promenade Deck Car Access P & S Sliding Doors. 4. First Class Smoke Room. 5. Inflatable Life Rafts. 6. Emergency Generator Room. 7. Radar Scanner. 8. Wheelhouse. 9. Engineers' and Officers' Accommodation. 10. Windlass. 11. Shelter Deck Upper Car Access P & S Sliding Doors. 12. Main Deck Car Access P & S Hinged Hydraulically Operated Doors (door not shown). 13. Shelter Deck Lower Car Access P & S Sliding Doors. 14. Shaft Space. 15. Sanitary and Fresh Water Pumps. 16. Main Deck Car Stowage. 17. Starboard Main Gearcase. 18. Starboard Main Steam Turbine. 19. 200-kW. Diesel Generator. 20. Stabilizer Fin. 21. Starboard Main Boiler. 22. Oil Fuel Bunkers. 23. First Class Lounge. 24. Second Class Lounge. 25. Main Deck For'd Car Access P & S (hinged hydraulically-operated doors).

The stern area of each vessel contained a sort of helter skelter spiral arrangement which allowed small vehicles to be driven aboard through a series of side doors at varying states of the tide without linkspans or bow and stern doors. It seemed quite clever at the time but nothing larger than a van could be carried.

Diesel-powered car ferries to the same principle appeared from 1971 and the earlier pair went in 1984–1985, thus bringing an end to steam power in the fleet.

As the car ferries began to arrive, the company still set great store on conventional excursion traffic both to and away from the Island. An amazing variety of one offs took place which some histories detail but whose surviving publicity ephemera, even from the 1960s, must be scarce.

Certain regular destinations got their own handbills and in 1965 the Irish ports of Belfast and Dublin provided examples. That to Dublin included the details of a connecting coach tour of the city. The interest in the Belfast one comes from the Ramsey call. The pier there had opened in 1886 and incorporated a tramway for passengers and their luggage from the start. *Manxman* carried out the last Steam Packet calls in September 1970.

THE ISLE OF MAN STEAM PACKET COMPANY LTD.
(Incorporated in the Isle of Man)

1965 DAY EXCURSIONS
TO
BELFAST

The Company may alter, withdraw, or curtail any service or suspend or cancel any sailing as the Company may think necessary.

STEAMER CALLS RAMSEY WEATHER PERMITTING

From DOUGLAS 08 30 hours
From RAMSEY   09 00 hours

From BELFAST 17 00 hours

JUNE — THURSDAY 17th
FRIDAYS 4th, 11th and 25th
JULY — EVERY TUESDAY AND FRIDAY
AUGUST — EVERY TUESDAY AND FRIDAY
SEPTEMBER — FRIDAYS 3rd and 10th

These Excursions allow about three hours ashore in Belfast

FARES: 1st Class 26/- ;   2nd Class 22/-

Children under 3 years of age FREE ; 3 years and under 14, Half-fare.
Infants must be accompanied by an adult.

All fares are current at time of publication and are liable to alteration without notice.

TICKETS, which may be purchased before the actual sailing day, can be obtained at :—
DOUGLAS **Booking and Enquiry Office, Sea Terminal Buildings, Victoria Pier, or
Imperial Buildings, The Quay.
Isle of Man Railway Enquiry Offices, Villa Marina and Palace, The Promenade.
W. H. Chapman, Ltd., Travel House, Victoria Street.
Paul Gelling and Partners, Duke Street.**
RAMSEY **Company's Office, The Quay.**
DAY EXCURSION PASSENGERS ARE NOT PERMITTED TO CARRY LUGGAGE.

Passengers and their accompanied luggage will only be carried subject to the Company's Standard Conditions of Carriage of Passengers and Passengers' Accompanied Property as exhibited in the Company's Offices and on board its vessels. Acceptance of a ticket issued by the Company binds the passenger to these Conditions.

Breakfasts, Luncheons, Teas and Refreshments can be obtained on board.
Imperial Buildings, Douglas.   A. J. FICK, General Manager.
January, 1965.

VICTORIA PRESS LTD., DOUGLAS

It was not just the mainland railway that provided connectional facilities and by the early 1980s; leaflets linking the Steam Packet into the National Express network existed like this 1981 issue for services from the Yorkshire and Lancashire towns.

As the company sought to beef its image up, some logo innovations took place. Isle of Man Steam Packet Seaways was one such and this wavy image appeared not only on the literature but on the hull sides. A version of it graced M.V. *Lady of Mann* and the 1984 brochure.

Although older material is always perceived as more interesting, in the case of the Steam Packet, there were so many changes in the 1980s, that much of interest can be found in that decade. In the early part of that decade the 1976 car ferry *Lady of Mann* took the honours on the covers of several of the annual brochures. These by now were A4 in size and a run from then onwards is an impressive collection. Adoption of an A4 brochure appears to have come late to the company. My earliest is 1980, I presently think this was the first.

Lady of Mann gave ground after 1984 to a new vessel in the light of the 1985 upheaval. The merger with Sea Containers took effect from 1 April 1985 at which time the Liverpool sailings were abandoned (for a while, and it was not until 1996 that Sea Containers gained a controlling stake). A new flagship M.V. *Mona's Isle* arrived a couple of days later only to have a short and unhappy association with the company. Later that year, through the Sealink link which Sea Containers brought, another vessel assumed that role.

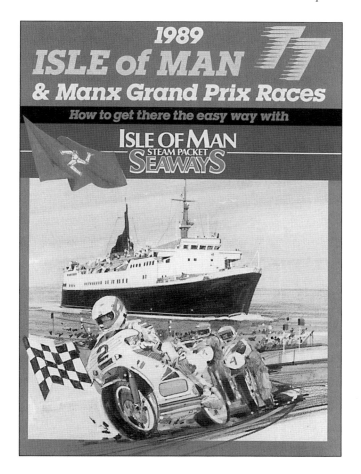

Return to the Stranraer chapter and the publicity for the M.V. *Antrim Princess* may be seen. Her late 1960s introductory publicity had not been of the best. Two decades later and as the M.V. *Tynwald*, she appeared all over Steam Packet literature. In the four years 1986–1990 lots of items featured her through photos, silhouettes on tiny A7 timetable cards and larger versions of that on BR leaflets for travel to the island. My selective collection finds her on the covers of eleven items.

That shown can rightly rank as amongst the nicest. Someone painted her for use on the 1989 TT and Grand Prix brochure. This was something of a change from what had been available in 1955 (look back to Fleetwood).

The artwork continued inside the eight page brochure with impressive imagery of the races and another impression of the ship. There was an historical summary of the sport in the island, a map of the course and full timetable details of the special sailings which covered Heysham, Liverpool and Belfast. The company had really moved with the times. The bikers no longer had to empty their machines of their petrol! Not too long to go and the Seacats would arrive (in 1994).

The leaflet might have been some consolation for the year before. In 1988, the Steam Packet was threatened by strikes at TT time, leaving the Manx Government to spend £1 million chartering Fred Olsen's M.V. *Bolette* as a stop-gap. How one itches for a leaflet about that! In the event the Steam Packet sailings resumed but the charter was still fulfilled.

Tradition had survived elsewhere in the company for many years. My journeys in the 1980s were met with the sort of carbonated coupon ticket that many shipping operators were using. Not too long before and a vast stock of Edmondson cards were used, numbers of which can still be obtained through the Transport Ticket Society in 2001.

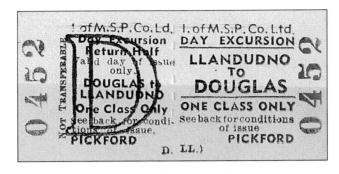

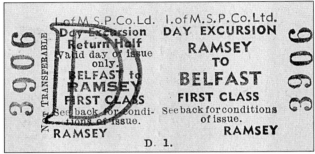

Some examples are the Llandudno-Douglas Day Excursion issued at the Pickford's travel agency in Llandudno, a similar ticket for a Ramsey-Belfast journey as covered by the handbill just illustrated and issued at the Ramsey I.O.M.S.P. Co. office to be seen imminently.

One of the two Liverpool journeys reveals that conference traffic was important, I.M.T.B. stands for Isle of Man Tourist Board. Stage on the last ticket refers to Liverpool Landing Stage as the point of issue.

This habit of issuing individual ticket stock to the point of sale added extra variety to an already involved stock. Possessing the relevant brochures listing the company's agents can help to reveal the locations and the appearance of B.I.S.P. Co. on Dublin originating tickets shows the B&I ferry office there to have been a Steam Packet agent.

Another long surviving exemple of the traditional company and an unusual concept in publicity was a series of model ships displayed on railway stations. One source states these were Bassett-Lowke made.

The model illustrated was on Blackburn station in 1984 – even then leaving an exhibition standard model in a showcase on a station seemed brave. Surely these must all have disappeared now? It is of the *Viking* in the fleet 1906–1954. She had been the company's first turbine steamer.

At varying times the author knows that models were also at Bolton, Morecambe, Manchester Victoria, Rhyl and Wolverhampton stations. One was on board Sealink's *Caesarea*, another in Midland Red's Nuneaton Travel Centre and more in various museums.

In July 1988 the erstwhile Ramsey office of the Steam Packet was looking neglected. It was some way from the pier being on the banks of the harbour formed by the Sulby River.

Perhaps having to gaze at the competition had proved too depressing? Ramsey Harbour had provided a haven for operators bent on challenging the Steam Packet. Those operators had had a bonanza earlier in 1988 when the Steam Packet had been strikebound for seven weeks.

As far back as 1913, discontent with the Steam Packet had led to the formation of the Ramsey Steamship Company whose 'Ben...' vessels the author was photographing in 1988. A relative newcomer which commenced in 1985 was Mezeron Ltd. With two ships, they offered a cargo and container service to Glasson Dock near Lancaster.

It can be seen that using Ramsey Harbour requires vessels to take the ground. Mezeron's M.V. *Silver River* moored behind the M.V. *Colby River* was bought after her first companion the M.V. *Sulby River* capsized and sunk off Ramsey in November 1985. Both the Mezeron and Ramsey companies were still active in 1995.

Passing the Isle of Man without stopping were the vessels of the Belfast Steamship Company on their way to Liverpool. They did this between 1852 and 1981. A number of company sponsored postcards are known. That of the T.S.S. *Patriotic* shows a significant vessel. The company had adopted the ___*ic* suffix in 1863, a tradition which lasted until the *Ulster Monarch* in 1929.

Patriotic, pictured on the opposite page, came from Harland & Wolff in 1912 to start eighteen years on the Liverpool run. She then moved to the B&I and their Dublin-Liverpool service. Both wars were spent as a troopship and then between 1947-1956 she metamorphosed into Coast Lines' cruise vessel with her fourth name *Lady Killarney*. As such she was found in a Scottish loch in the author's previous book *To Western Scottish Waters*. Her replacement in effect, for it was a BR vessel, has been met at Heysham.

Some dramatic colour postcards of Belfast Steamship Co. ships appeared over a considerable period, some sharing the use of John S. Smith artwork. His work has been met with sister company Burns & Laird in the Glasgow chapter. Smith had illustrated their versions

of the Coast Lines standard motor ships. This series had been started with the Belfast Steamship Company's 1929 *Ulster Monarch* and Smith's card of her is reproduced as illustration 12 of the colour section.

With its reverse references to 'Ulster Imperial Line', this is surely a pre-war image? That heading had appeared on the company's timetables and other publicity from 1929, the year when the ___*ic* naming tradition was broken.

Other cards of the *Ulster Monarch* dated to the 1930s are known from the noted marine artist Harry Hudson Rodmell. Smith's work was used well into the 1950s when the 1955 freighter *Ulster Pioneer* received a card. Company pride was considerable although that attractive vessel was out of date at her launch.

Looking at 1960 as in the timetable brochure (illustration 10 of the colour section), the Belfast Steamship Co. remained an exemplar of tradition. *Ulster Monarch* and *Ulster Prince* had been the last word in modernity in 1929, albeit linked to the backward looking imperial concept in their marketing. Incredibly these 1929 and 1938 veterans still had another six years to go on the crossing having been considerably refitted in 1957/1960 respectively. Inside, the brochure detailed BR connections arriving at any of the three mainline termini then open but not at the adjacent Riverside. As with several of the Coast Lines routes, much of the publicity unavoidably focused on the night due to the sailing pattern: Burns & Laird and B&I furnish other examples.

These night services throughout the Irish Sea became an inspiration to folk music. Familiar songs like *The Rocky Road to Dublin* or *The Night Ferry Has Taken Me Home Again* sung by The Fureys all recall the steamers' voyages.

For further information apply :—

Belfast Steamship Company Ltd.

9 Donegall Place   **42 Donegall Quay**
BELFAST

Phone : 23636   Phone : 20211
Grams: "Passenger" Telex: 74546 Grams: "Basalt"

COAST LINES Ltd. (Agents)

BIRMINGHAM, 4   **108 Dale End**
Grams : "Coastwise"   Phone : Central 3612

BRISTOL, 1   **The Grove**
Grams : "Coastwise"   Phone : Bristol 21142

CARDIFF   **York Warehouse,**
                    East Side, East Dock
Grams : "Coastwise"   Phone : Cardiff 26511

LEEDS, 1   **74 Wellington Street**
Grams : "Coastwise"   Phone : Leeds 21106

LIVERPOOL, 2   **Reliance House**
                         Water Street
Grams : "Afloat"   Phone : Central 3381
          Telex : 62293

LONDON, W.1   **227 Regent Street**
Grams: "Comfyships Wesdo" Phone: Regent 6627

MANCHESTER, 2   **10 Tib Lane,**
                         Cross Street
Grams : "Pebble"   Phone : Deansgate 6166

PLYMOUTH   **Wallsend House,**
                         Derry's Cross
Grams : "Colonial"   Phone : Plymouth 62589

SOUTHAMPTON   **Seaway House,**
                         Town Quay
Grams: "Coastwise" Phone: Southampton 22151

SWANSEA   **Exchange Buildings**
Grams : "Coastwise"   Phone : Swansea 52016

or any office of the Motoring Associations

Take your
CAR
with you to
NORTHERN
IRELAND

via
LIVERPOOL
by
BELFAST
STEAMSHIP
COMPANY LIMITED

Back with Belfast Steamship, the company could not ignore the kettle on the boil. Cars wanted to get to and from Northern Ireland. They could be carried on the overnight service as this 1961 leaflet demonstrates, the snag being that for the 9.30 p.m. sailing, the motorist had to deposit their car at the dock gate by 4 p.m. Nor would cars be carried on certain peak dates like mid-July. Interestingly the ship on the cover appears to be M.V. *Scottish Coast* and not one of the regular pair. When new in 1957 and again at different times in the 1960s, she had significant spells on the service.

Some simple reckoning with the fares will reveal what a cost shipping a car this way was. The basic second class fare was £1 10s, a cabin added 10s. An eleven-foot car cost £7 10s to ship.

1. Clyde Shipping Co. off Arran, postcard Image. (See page 23).

2. R.M.S. *Princess Maud* leaving Loch Ryan. (See page 38).

3 & 4. Details from the Burns and Laird Line Glasgow to Belfast cover. (See page 36).

5. The Clyde Shipping Co. *Fastnet* itinerary. (See page 24).

6. Burns & Laird's 'Drive Through Car Ferry' Ardrossan–Belfast front cover. (See page 27).

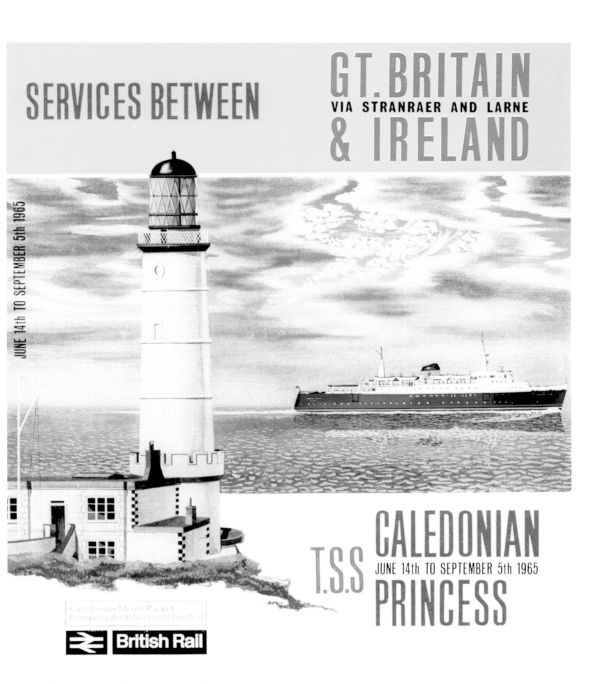

7. *Caledonian Princess* Summer 1965 brochure. (See page 45).

8. Isle of Man for everyone
Season 1959 cover. (See
page 85).

9. Isle of Man 1958 Summer Services cover. (See page 85).

10. Belfast Steamship Co. 1960
timetable. (See page 95.)

11. Coastal cruises by Coast Line Ltd. (See page 104).

LIVERPOOL 2. Reliance House, Water Street
Telephone: Central 3381 *Tele*
LONDON, W.1. 227 Regent S
Telephone: Regent 6627 *Tele*
BIRMINGHAM 2. Neville Ho
BRISTOL 1. The Grove
CARDIFF. 9 Cory's Building
FALMOUTH. Falmouth Wha
LEEDS 1. Yorkshire House,
MANCHESTER 2. 10 Tib La
PLYMOUTH. Wallsend Hou
SOUTHAMPTON. Seaway H
SWANSEA. Exchange Build
BELFAST. Belfast S.S. Co.
CORK. City of Cork S. P. C
DUBLIN. British & Irish S. P
GLASGOW C2. Burns & Lai
NEWCASTLE-UPON-TYNE.
OR PRINCIPAL TRAVEL A

Coast Lin

coastal cruises

by Coast Lines Ltd

12. M.V. *Ulster Monarch*. (See page 95).

13. S.S. *Cambria*. (See page 109).

14. *Irish Mail* centenary brochure. (See page 108).

British Railways

LONDON MIDLAND REGION

IRISH CAR FERRY
HANDBOOK

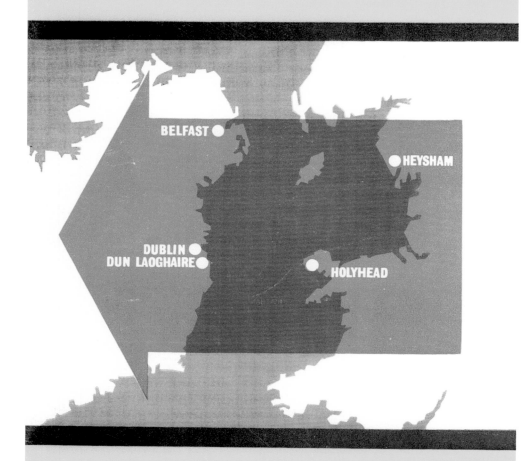

BELFAST ●

● HEYSHAM

DUBLIN ●
DUN LAOGHAIRE ●

HOLYHEAD ●

SERVICES AND FARES 1965

15. *Opposite:* Irish Car Ferry Handbook cover. (See page 121).

16. *This page:* London Midland Railway's Container Services to Dublin 1962 cover. (See page 125).

17. BR Irish Services Timetables summer 1954. (See page 138).

IRISH CROSS CHANNEL
TIMETABLES

15th JUNE TO 13th SEPTEMBER 1959
OR UNTIL FURTHER NOTICE

18. BR Irish Services Timtables 1959. (See page 138).

19. The pleasure is yours in Southern Ireland 24 May 1965. (See page 146).

20. One of the pull outs from the above leaflet.

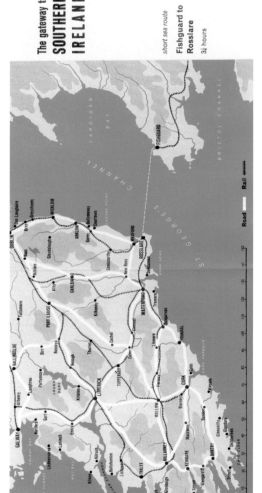

Proper roll on/roll off facilities (and containerised freight) was the only answer. A new M.V. *Ulster Prince* and M.V. *Ulster Queen* provided the answer for the vehicles from April 1967.

Some effort went into the launch publicity. The item above with its composite artwork cover is a four side flimsy introducing the new ships: it is not their first timetable. Stern doors only were fitted and turntables and passenger lifts were used in the garage. 120 cars and some coaches could be carried. The traditional overnight sailings were retained.

Comparison with the material marking the arrival of the *Lion* at Ardrossan suggests that the same designer was used but the items are obstinately anonymous. The Liver Building and new BR electric engine then appearing on the London-Liverpool service add context.

Inside an unknown's artist work in painting the new vessels appeared. Harland & Wolff and Cammell Laird each built one.

The two 1967 ships were to command the service until November 1981. In their last years, they were in P&O Ferries' blue and by then, the service was in a sorry state finally collapsing with strikes and a crew 'sit-in'. A sad end to the hopes that had accompanied their introduction. The troubled 1970s were not the best time to be trying to run a service to Ulster out of Liverpool, there were just too many headaches in the combination.

BELFAST STEAMSHIP CO. LTD. | DRIVE-ON/DRIVE OFF m.v. "ULSTER QUEEN" and "ULSTER PRINCE" NIGHT SAILINGS LIVERPOOL—BELFAST FOR PASSENGERS, CARS AND UNITISED CARGO

BURNS & LAIRD LINES LTD. | DRIVE-THROUGH m.v. "LION" DAILY SAILINGS ARDROSSAN—BELFAST FOR PASSENGERS, CARS AND COMMERCIAL VEHICLES

In those fourteen years there was much publicity produced. From 1971, P&O owned the Belfast Steamship Co. and this was reflected in the publicity. Among the smallest items were playing card-sized (or A7) calendars for free distribution – often to business contacts. Various Coast Lines companies produced these, but so did BR's Irish Sea shipping and Caledonian MacBrayne. The calendar would occupy one side, and images of the ships the other.

This 1972 offering joins the two Coast Lines Irish Sea car ferry services in the one view putting together M.V.s *Lion* and *Ulster Queen*. A leaflet from the same period twinning the two routes appears in the Ardrossan entries.

Despite the losses and aggravation that the service had met with under P&O, a link between Belfast and Liverpool was too important to lose. Indeed the sit-ins on the two ferries were only ended with the promise of a new operator in the wings.

Notably the muscle behind the link came with financing from the Republic's Irish Shipping and Allied Irish Bank. The result was a Northern Ireland company Belfast Car Ferries operating Irish Shipping's 1973 vessel the M.V. *St Patrick* now re-named *Saint Colum 1*.

That is the ferry seen from the air on the cover of this 1983 leaflet. The service started in May 1982. The parent company then spent some years in financial difficulty before being transformed into Irish Continental in 1987 parenting Belfast Car Ferries and Irish Ferries.

That last name holds the clue to the next step. B&I was taken over by Irish Ferries in 1991 and the title was adopted for all operations in 1995.

The Belfast Car Ferries operation had ceased in October 1990. For some months, the route was entirely defunct as far as passengers and cars went. In the summer of 1991 a service of sorts was offered by the Isle of Man Steam Packet.

The baton passed to Norse Irish Ferries, who in 1992 opened a passenger service (following on from a freight service) between Belfast-Liverpool. It was still operating as the millennium ended and a variety of attractive leaflets have existed like this 1996 issue.

M.V. *Norse Lagan* is the ferry featured, she is a 1968 vessel originally built and used in Canada. She initiated the service for Norse Irish but by 1998 was replaced by the M.V.s *Lagan Viking* and the *Mersey Viking*.

Something to anticipate as I write will be a new tranche of material due in 2002 when what is now the Norse Merchant service shifts to a new terminal: the £22 million Twelve Quays project at Birkenhead.

Services to Dublin from Liverpool would evidently be as important as those to Belfast. B&I bought out the 1824 founded City of Dublin Steam Packet in 1920 and with it their Liverpool-Dublin service, their Dun Laoghaire-Holyhead service was a mail contract and had been lost to the LNWR.

This 1954 leaflet (above, left) presents the route at the core of its Coast Lines period. The crossing was a familiar (if you have started at the beginning) nightly service producing a night image for the cover. That is unsigned but it is is not dis-similar to the John S. Smith work already seen.

The vessel ploughing through the Irish Sea is a typical Coast Lines standard motor packet. The name cannot be read which may be intentional but we can be sure that the two 1948 sisters *Munster* and *Leinster* are portrayed. Four successive generations of *Munster* and *Leinsters* operated the route, all were motorships. The 1937 pair came first, though before them there were the steam *Lady Leinster* and the *Lady Munster*. The 1948 pair carried on the traditional overnight service out of Princes Dock to Dublin North Wall. A note in this leaflet implies that the bus link from Princes Dock (for the adjacent Liverpool Riverside was not used) to the Liverpool stations was undertaken in B&I's own buses. Any dedicated ephemera for them would be a catch. The note said this was a free service so that quest might be a struggle.

Over the period 1967-1969, the third generation replaced the 1948 vessels and the terminal was moved to Carrier's Dock, Liverpool, and a new car ferry berth in Dublin. Yes, roll on/roll off had arrived and a day sailing was added. The operation was by now an Irish state-owned company. Did that assist the Verolme Cork Dockyard to gain the M.V. *Leinster* contract which in 1969 became the first roll on/roll off channel ferry to be built in the Republic?

These ships were forward thinking with both bow and stern doors and able to turn around 220 cars in an hour.

A good example of a swinging sixties brochure with ample artwork was available at the outset. Two views of the new ships were given, and both had the name *B+I Motorway*. The service did not stay at Carrier's Wharf long, which dates early brochures.

The fourth generation appeared in 1979-1981 although tradition was broken in that a *Connacht* was substituted for a *Munster*. Through the 1970s, B&I's partner route to Dublin-Liverpool was Cork-Swansea and one brochure covered both, so move to Swansea for a further viewing.

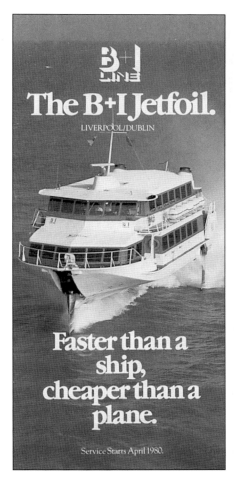

A fascinating series of changes took place in the 1980s on the Liverpool-Dublin service. An early attempt at a high-speed ferry was one. B&I commenced a passenger jetfoil to supplement the car ferries in April 1980 and this is the launch leaflet. It is readily apparent how small the vessel was. A three-hour crossing at 50mph was scheduled and my anxious mind wonders how akin the whole thing was to travel in an out-of-control minibus? The leaflet would have had none of that promising a comfortable seat and a duty free drink, but surely it must have been easy to have felt quite exposed? The leaflet claimed that the 'Jetfoil can sail in just about all conditions'. Despite this, the weather did lead to cancellations and the service did not endure. Instead B&I suffered huge losses in the early 1980s, more than £7 million in 1981.

Similar Boeing hydrofoils appeared on services from London, Brighton and Newhaven and were equally shortlived. Their only UK service with some success was from Dover to Ostend for which publicity over a number of years is relatively easy to find.

The short lived Irish Sea operation makes this associated leaflet issued by British Railways in the summer of 1980 all the more interesting. A rear view of the vessel is given and the Gaelic name is visible: *Cún na mara* means 'Hound of the Sea'. On the side is a Boeing Jetfoil slogan not visible in the previous view. The leaflet could hardly be more inconsequential, printed on one side only, but what a find from only twenty years ago.

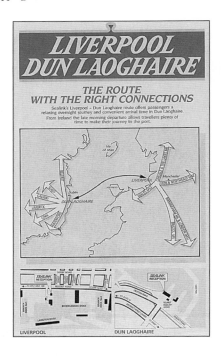

Over the last thirty years a stream of glossy A4 travel brochures have piled out from the ferry operators. Often of evident attraction, their bulk, repetitiveness and sheer number will probably put most people off retaining any quantity. Storage cost may far outway acquisition cost.

For those reasons alone, what was rubbish one day is a collectable the next, or at least by the next decade. Such is the pace of change, that the apparent repetitivenes might be just that, an unsustained opinion because numbers of these items represent something very unusual.

The simple presence of the Sea Container's Sealink image visible on the exterior with the officer's sleeve ring/S and L merged for Sealink symbol limits the item above to 1984–1990. Inside the same holds good with a white-hulled outline drawing of M.V. *Earl William* in Sealink British Ferries colours. That drawing alone will quicken the pace for the *cognoscenti* as will the whole idea of a Sealink Liverpool-Dun Laoghaire service, a thought anchored by the cover announcement 'New Service 1988'.

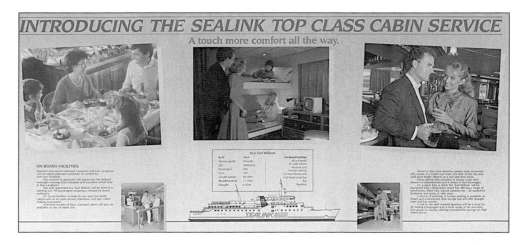

All sorts of unlikely bedfellows: *Earl William* had started life in 1964 as Thoresen's *Viking II*. She entered the Sealink fleet as *Earl William* in 1977. Her home for the next decade was the Channel Island services until 1987 found her in use as a prison ship at Harwich. Then the Liverpool-Dun Laoghaire service came about from 25 April 1988.

Sealink at Liverpool was a complete innovation but it was a consequence of B&I withdrawing their route in 1987, another unimaginable thought. The last years of B&I saw their two routes being Pembroke-Rosslare and Holyhead-Dun Laoghaire. Sealink's new service did not work out and ended in January 1990 making the few pieces of individual publicity instantly noteworthy. Whilst it lasted, its problems included an on-board bank robbery, mechanical breakdown and strike action.

A Liverpool-Dublin car ferry link was in place in 2000. The service commenced in March 1998 and is an impressive example of how the latest high-speed ferries change things. The *Superseacat* is actually a high-speed monohull. Four water jets power her at 38 knots carrying 165 cars between the two cities in just under four hours. A futuristic journey delivered by James Sherwood's Sea Containers which parents the Seacat operation. *Earl William* took eight to nine hours.

The brochure shown is another one of those recent A4s which it would be so easy to ignore, the more so since 1998 saw three editions of this one brochure, each with the same cover. That shown is the key launch issue: Edition One for the new route. After three seasons the *Superseacat Three* monohull gave way to the Incat *Rapide* catamaran brought in from the Dover crossing by Sea Containers. In its time on the route the *Superseacat Three* had shifted 144,000 vehicles.

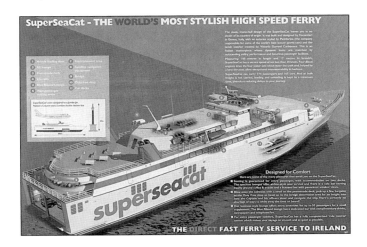

Over the same period P&O have been developing a Liverpool-Dublin service. this received a new vessel, the M.V. *European Ambassador* for 2001, only for that year to see a shock announcement that the service would move to Mostyn in the Dee Estuary. That service started on 19 November 2001.

I suspect that Kelly colliers never carried passengers but it was not only Clyde Shipping (see the Glasgow entries) whose coasters did seek out passengers.

Readers may have understood that most of Coast Lines' publicity was issued in the name of its subsidiaries. Coast Lines itself operated coasters and they did not attract much publicity.

Coast Lines issued the publicity for the Liverpool-Western Scotland cruises illustrated in *To Western Scottish Waters*. Additionally a number of their coasters were prepared to take passengers. This was an old established tradition which the 1960s put paid to. At the start of the decade this arrangement covered London-Liverpool with calls at Irish and British south coast ports. The actual Coast Lines fleet then stood at nineteen vessels. By 1971 the passenger sailings had gone and the now P&O owned Coast Lines was down to five ships.

All of which makes the survival of the folder for the Liverpool-London sailings, reproduced as illustration 11 of the colour section, of some interest. Undated but likely to be within a few years either side of 1960, the classic bridge amidships coaster features in the binoculars. The reverse used the same concept but with London's Tower Bridge and Liverpool's Anglican Cathedral in view.

The round trip took ten days and inside the brochure monochrome illustrations and text revealed the two vessels used to be the *Caledonian Coast* and *Hibernian Coast*. These bridge-amidships motor vessels dated from 1947-1948.

From Liverpool, there remains one other significant group of local passenger sailings out into the Irish Sea. These provided the links to, and often the cruises from, the North Wales seaside resorts.

Between 1891 and 1962, these services were the province of the Liverpool & North Wales Steamship Company amongst whose ships various generations of the *St Seiriol*, *St Trillo* and the *St Tudno* became institutionalised.

PLEASE RETAIN THIS PROGRAMME FOR REFERENCE

PROGRAMME

OF

ORDINARY RETURN TICKETS

TO

LLANDUDNO

AND

MENAI BRIDGE

VIA LIVERPOOL AND THE LIVERPOOL & NORTH WALES S.S. Co.'s STEAMERS
WEATHER AND OTHER CIRCUMSTANCES PERMITTING

WEEKDAYS

8th June to 16th September 1957

SUNDAYS

9th June to 15th September 1957

where train service permits

BRITISH RAILWAYS

E 46

BRITISH RAILWAYS

ORDINARY RETURN TICKETS

TO

LLANDUDNO

AND

MENAI BRIDGE

VIA

LIVERPOOL AND THE LIVERPOOL & NORTH WALES S.S. CO.'S STEAMERS

WEEKDAYS and SUNDAYS

Where Train Service Permits

8th June to 16th September 1957

INCLUSIVE

AVAILABILITY

BY ANY TRAIN TO LIVERPOOL, IN CONNECTION WITH THE LIVERPOOL AND NORTH WALES S.S. Co.'s STEAMERS DEPARTING LIVERPOOL Prince's Landing Stage AT 10.45 a.m. weather and other circumstances permitting. LLANDUDNO DUE 1.5 p.m. MENAI BRIDGE DUE 2.40 p.m.

ANY DAY WITHIN THREE MONTHS FROM AND INCLUDING THE DATE OF ISSUE, BY LIVERPOOL AND NORTH WALES S.S.'s STEAMER FROM MENAI BRIDGE AT 3.45 p.m. AND LLANDUDNO AT 5.15 p.m. DUE LIVERPOOL Prince's Landing Stage 7.40 p.m. PROCEEDING FROM LIVERPOOL TO DESTINATION BY FIRST AVAILABLE SERVICE. It will be necessary for Passengers Returning after 16th September to Travel by Rail, paying the Supplementary Charges shown below.

PRIVATE CABINS MAY BE BOOKED IN ADVANCE
DINING SALOONS, CAFETERIA AND REFRESHMENTS BARS ON BOARD
For Booking Stations and Fares see Pages 2 and 3

INTERCHANGE—BOAT AND RAIL ARRANGEMENTS
Passengers holding Period Steamer Tickets have the option of returning by rail on surrendering return Half Boat Ticket and on payment of the undermentioned rates.
LLANDUDNO—5s. 10d.   From MENAI BRIDGE or BANGOR—7s. 6d.

Children under three years of age, free ; three years and under fourteen, half-fares.

tickets are issued subject to the British Transport Commission's published Regulations and applicable to British Railways exhibited at their Stations or obtainable free of charge at Station Offices.

TICKETS CAN BE OBTAINED IN ADVANCE AT STATIONS AND OFFICIAL RAILWAY AGENTS

Further information will be supplied on application to the Stations, Official Railway Agents, or to Mr. T. W. POLDING, District Passenger Manager, L.M.R., Hunts Bank, Manchester, 3. Tel. No. BLAckfriars 3456, Ext. 587 or 566.

January 1957   BR 35008/1

Published by British Railways (London Midland Region) 1/57 Printed in Gt. Britain Jowett & Sowry Ltd., Leeds, 1

Just as the Clyde shipbuilder Denny found a market for its products by actually operating the Forth Ferry, so the L.& N.W.S.S. Co. was actually a front for Fairfield's of Govan who built the ships.

Our inspection of their publicity comes from the final decade, but how fortunate it is that even these items have survived. The first item is issued by the shipping company itself and appears typical of their later handbills. The piece is very similiar to a railway handbill and as the timetable makes clear through bookings from railway stations were an important trade. The artwork depicts their largest vessel, the 1926 *St Tudno* which stayed in the fleet till the end. Reference to a one shilling souvenir guide is tantalising.

Similar artwork appeared on many British Railways-issued handbills. Above is the cover of a four side affair which was issued each summer and showed the huge range of stations from the North West which issued through bookings: Accrington to Wyre Dock.

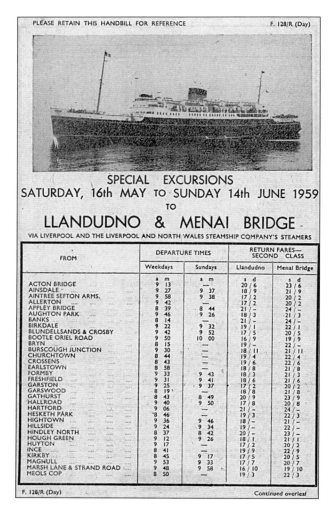

PLEASE RETAIN THIS HANDBILL FOR REFERENCE   F. 128/R (Day)

SPECIAL EXCURSIONS
SATURDAY, 16th MAY TO SUNDAY 14th JUNE 1959
TO
LLANDUDNO & MENAI BRIDGE
VIA LIVERPOOL AND THE LIVERPOOL AND NORTH WALES STEAMSHIP COMPANY'S STEAMERS

FROM	DEPARTURE TIMES		RETURN FARES— SECOND CLASS	
	Weekdays	Sundays	Llandudno	Menai Bridge
	a m	a m	s d	s d
ACTON BRIDGE	9 13	—	20 / 6	23 / 6
AINSDALE	9 27	9 37	18 / 9	21 / 9
AINTREE SEFTON ARMS.	9 58	9 38	17 / 2	20 / 2
ALLERTON	9 42	—	17 / 2	20 / 2
APPLEY BRIDGE	8 39	8 44	21 / –	24 / –
AUGHTON PARK	9 46	9 26	18 / 3	21 / 3
BANKS	8 14	—	21 / –	24 / –
BIRKDALE	9 22	9 32	19 / 1	22 / 1
BLUNDELLSANDS & CROSBY	9 42	9 52	17 / 5	20 / 5
BOOTLE ORIEL ROAD	9 50	10 00	16 / 9	19 / 9
BRYN	8 15	—	19 / –	22 / –
BURSCOUGH JUNCTION	9 30	—	18 / 11	21 / 11
CHURCHTOWN	8 44	—	19 / 4	22 / 4
CROSSENS	8 43	—	19 / 6	22 / 6
EARLSTOWN	8 58	—	18 / 8	21 / 8
FORMBY	9 33	9 43	18 / 3	21 / 3
FRESHFIELD	9 31	9 41	18 / 6	21 / 6
GARSTON	9 25	9 37	17 / 2	20 / 2
GARSWOOD	19 —	—	18 / 8	21 / 8
GATHURST	8 43	8 49	20 / 9	23 / 9
HALLROAD	9 40	9 50	17 / 8	20 / 8
HARTFORD	9 06	—	21 / –	24 / –
HESKETH PARK	8 46	—	19 / 3	22 / 3
HIGHTOWN	9 36	9 46	18 / –	21 / –
HILLSIDE	9 24	9 34	19 / –	22 / –
HINDLEY NORTH	8 37	8 42	20 / –	23 / –
HOUGH GREEN	9 12	9 26	18 / 1	21 / 1
HUYTON	9 17	—	17 / 2	20 / 2
INCE	8 41	—	19 / 9	22 / 9
KIRKBY	8 45	9 17	17 / 5	20 / 5
MAGHULL	9 53	9 33	17 / 7	20 / 7
MARSH LANE & STRAND ROAD	9 48	9 58	16 / 10	19 / 10
MEOLS COP	8 50	—	19 / 3	22 / 3

F. 128/R (Day)   Continued overleaf

Occasionally things went astray. This handbill issued for the early season of 1959 showed one from BR's Holyhead pair of 1949 motorships.

When the L.&N.W.S.S. Co. sailings ceased, the Isle of Man Steam Packet stepped in from the 1963 season with replacements running from Douglas and Liverpool to Llandudno. During 1967 the state of Llandudno pier caused a temporary cessation and thereafter the story of North Wales services is best described as variable. 1980 was the last year the Steam Packet operated from Liverpool-Llandudno. Other operators have also tried. In 1982 the highspeed *Highland Seabird* encountered in *To Western Scottish Waters* working for Western Ferries gave it a go. More recently *Waverley* or *Balmoral* have offered programmes.

Back in the final years of the L.&N.W.S.S. Co. through bookings were also the excuse for bus company literature to feature the steamers (opposite). The different drawing was clearly intended to show *St Tudno* leaving Llandudno.

These Ribble leaflets were, I assume, issued each year and for sure, there were a series covering various centres of Ribble operations. The problem of leaving the passengers to make their own way to the Landing Stage at Liverpool was no different whether it was a bus or a rail company.

Naturally when ships were wrecked, the companies were loath to publicise matters, but commercial photographers could see an opportunity for a postcard if the result happened to be photographable. This was the case with the 1876 P.S. *Rhos Neigr* which on the 20th July 1908 struck a rock in Penrhyn Bay and had to be beached and abandoned.

She had latterly been a locally owned vessel providing trips from Rhyl. It was a Mr Booth, Photographer, Colwyn Bay who seized the opportunity. The card had been posted on 8 August 1908 and its sender wrote of the wreck 'I do not think much of it'!

R I B B L E

Ref. No. 8230

in conjunction with

THE LIVERPOOL AND NORTH WALES STEAMSHIP Co. Ltd.

●

THROUGH BOOKINGS TO

LLANDUDNO and MENAI BRIDGE

by Ribble Regular Services and Turbine Steamers St. Tudno and St. Seiriol

DAILY SATURDAY, 24th MAY, to THURSDAY, 11th SEPTEMBER, 1958

Weather and circumstances permitting—subject to alteration without notice.

DAY EXCURSIONS ALLOW 4 HOURS ASHORE AT LLANDUDNO
OR 1 HOUR AT MENAI BRIDGE

FROM	Time Depart a.m.	COMBINED COACH—BOAT ADULT FARES (including Pier Tolls Liable to Alteration				Excursion Day Return	
		Ordinary				Llandudno (B)	Menai Bridge
		Llandudno		Menai Bridge			
		S	PR	S	PR		
SOUTHPORT, BUS STN. ...	8NSu50	11/10	19/-	13/10	21/6	17/-	19/
Birkdale, Crown Hotel ...	8NSu57	11/6	18/10	13/6	21/4	16/10	19/
Freshfield, Jct. By Pass Road and Liverpool Road	9NSu07	11/3	18/5	13/3	20/11	16/5	18/
Formby, Jct. By Pass Road and Altcar Road...	9NSu10	11/2	18/4	13/2	20/10	16/4	18/
Thornton, Virgins Lane ...	9NSu21	10/9	17/6	12/9	20/-	15/6	18/
(A) Liverpool, Skelhorne Street	9NSu47	←Coach arrive				Coach de	
(A) LIVERPOOL, Princes Landing Stage ...	10 45	←Boat depart				Boat due to ar	

S—Single.　　PR—Period Return.　　NSu—Not on Sunda
Children over 3 and under 14—approx. half Adult fare.

A—Passengers make their own way at own expense in each direction between Street Bus Terminus and Liverpool, Princes Landing Stage.
B—On certain Mondays, Thursdays and Sundays special Half-Day Excu Llandudno Only (ex Liverpool 2-0 p.m. — due back at Liverpool 9-0 5/- cheaper (See Steamship Company's separate announcements).

Book in advance at
RIBBLE BUS AND COACH STATION, LORD STREET, SOUTHPORT. Phon
Ribble vouchers for steamer must be exchanged at the Liverpool and North Wale Company's Office alongside the steamer.

Ribble Motor Services Ltd., Frenchwood, Preston. Phone 4272.
Liverpool & North Wales Steamship Co. Ltd., 40 Chapel St., Liverpool, 3. Phone C

H. 2M. 5/58.

Catering on the Steamers . . .

Catering on the St. Tudno and the St. Seiriol is of a high standard and excellent meals are served. The dining saloons, cafeteria, refreshment bars and lounges are equipped on up-to-date lines and decorated in a pleasing style.

BOTH VESSELS ARE FULLY LICENSED

—◆《X》◆—

Private Parties and Works Outings

Reduced fares are available on the steamers for organised parties (Fridays excepted, June and September). You can obtain an inclusive quotation at any Ribble office for the private hire of luxury coaches from your home town to and from Liverpool and a cruise to either Llandudno or Menai Bridge. Reservations can be made in the dining saloon for parties requiring meals and special menus can be quoted if required.

Tickets are issued and passengers are carried subject to the General Passenger Regulations and Conditions of the respective operators as set out in their published time tables and available for reference at their various offices.

Five

The London and North Western and Holyhead

The Liverpool and North Wales Steamship Company services of the last chapter reached Menai Bridge on Anglesey.

On the opposite side of the island lies the smaller Holy Island where the port of Holyhead was adopted by the Queen's Packet of Queen Elizabeth I in the 1570s. Tales were handed down of terrible journeys by land and by sea in the course of getting from London to Dublin via Holyhead. Dean Swift in around 1713 waited a week at Holyhead for fair weather for the crossing and it was not a pleasant wait!

Development did not wait on the railway's arrival, as everyone should know of the wonders Telford did to today's A5 culminating in the 1826 Menai Strait bridge. Both the roads and the harbours were being improved. The South Stack Lighthouse at Holyhead opened in 1809.

Doubtless some official repository (or some very lucky private collector) will possess ephemera from the days of the horse drawn coach and the sailing packet.

From the author's collection matters start with the railway and the steamer. The former reached Holyhead on 1 August 1848. The Britannia Bridge was not complete for another two years so the 1970 closure was not the first time that rail passengers found their journey broken.

Nonetheless 1 August 1848 was the date that the famed *Irish Mail* train left Euston for the first time – the first truly named train in Britain.

That assertive fact and the accompanying image come from the attractive Centenary souvenir of the *Irish Mail* which is shown as illustration 14 of the colour section. Anniversaries are often the occasion for an attractive piece of official publicity and despite the austerity era and the newly nationalised industry, the *Centenary of the Irish Mail 1848-1948* written by V. Stewart Haram and published by The Railway Executive London Midland Region is just such a piece.

It illustrated (opposite, top) the P.S. *St Columba*, an Admiralty steam and sailing packet commissioned with three sisters in 1848 for the new service. The Admiralty ran the night service with the mails, the railway opened a day service with ships that were named *Cambria* and *Hibernia*, the first of many on the route. This twin operator situation paved the way for the City of Dublin Steam Packet to succeed to the mail contract in 1850 which anchored the two players at Holyhead until 1920.

That was the situation in the early years of the twentieth century. A third generation of *Cambria* had arrived from Denny of Dumbarton in 1897 and she was in place to feature in one of the earliest large-scale marketing crazes. Picture postcard production and collecting took off in the early 1900s in the wake of changes to postal legislation. *Picture Postcard Magazine* was first published in July 1900. The railway companies were early exponents of this media seeing valuable publicity opportunities and even a profitable sideline.

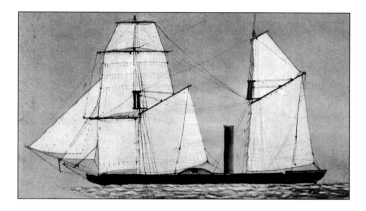

These 'official' postcards are nowadays sought after. Of the companies that issued them, the London & North Western was the most prolific. In under twenty years from 1904 around 1,000 different cards appeared. A substantial number related to the Irish Sea crossings that the company was interested in from Holyhead to Dublin, to Greenore and the Fleetwood services. Many of the cards were in 2d for six card sets and as they were reprinted, the reverse carried a slogan referring to the number of cards in millions sold. The figure of eleven million was reached. A copy of Alsop's catalogue is essential if you want to see how many Irish Sea subjects can be sought. The LNWR cards included other company's steamers as subjects like the Belfast Steamship Company vessels.

The S.S. *Cambria* card (illustration 13 of the colour section) is Alsop's LNW535 one of sixteen cards listed in the 'LNWR Steamships' set, a heading that far from exhausts coverage of the subject by the company. The card with its Britannia motif and McCorquodale printer's name on the reverse dates to around 1906-1907. Other relevant set titles include 'To Ireland via Holyhead' and 'Dublin and Holyhead'.

The 1897 *Cambria* became the *Arvonia* in 1920. This was to release the name for another new Denny-built T.S.S. *Cambria*. Whereas the previous *Cambria* had been built to work to Dublin North Wall, the 1920-1921 generation were purchased to operate the newly taken over mail service to Dun Laoghaire. *Cambria* and her three sisters could manage 25 knots.

The 1921 vessel just made British Railways ownership and was shown in the 1948 *Irish Mail* Centenary booklet with this illustration below. At the time a new motorship *Cambria* was in prospect illustrated later in this chapter.

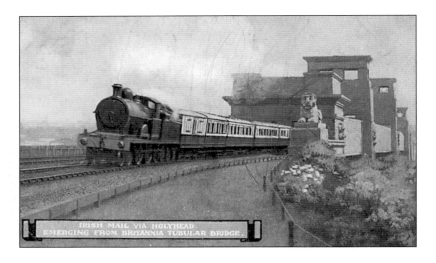

Just as there is a long list of shipping LNWR postcards, there is a similar range of cards featuring the *Irish Mail* train. The 'Express Trains' set of twenty-two cards had three views of the *Irish Mail* and others of the *Irish Day Express*. Shown is one of the three, Alsop's LNW225. The location is unmistakable and hardly needs a caption. Robert Stephenson's 1850 Britannia Bridge over the Menai Strait was the fundamental link that completed the London-Dublin chain. The trains passed through wrought iron tubes. As the years passed these were repeatedly pitched to protect the metalwork, an action which was to prove their undoing. That was far in the future in the later Edwardian years when this '9¼ millions sold' card appeared.

The LNWR was keen to make much of the ease of transfer between train and ship at Holyhead. Indeed it appears far easier than things in today's security encumbered climate. It helped that the British Isles were largely one nation at the time. There were several cards on this theme showing train, ship and Edwardian fashion. This is Alsop's LNW627 card from the 'To Ireland Via Holyhead' set. These cross-platform arrangements at Holyhead's Inner Harbour had been completed in 1880.

Many LNWR cards had Irish subjects, often far from their Dublin port facilities. Prior to 1909, the LNWR's Dublin interests were centered at North Wall on the River Liffey. This view shows the scene from the south bank with the LNWR steamers of the 1897 generation tied up at North Wall. The card comes from the 'City of Dublin' set.

There was an LNWR hotel at North Wall and, from 1877, their own railway station. In 1909 and 1920 passenger services moved to Dun Laoghaire but North Wall remained an important freight facility throughout British Railways days.

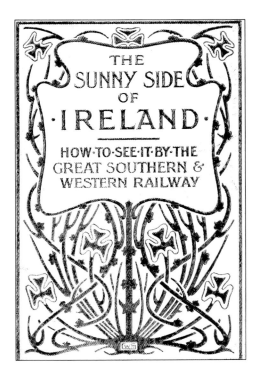

As far as passengers were concerned, there were two main flows. Emigrants and related traffic out of Ireland (which did not attract spectacular publicity) and – as one focus of the postcard sales – tourism to the Emerald Isle. Companies based in Ireland were fully alive to the possibility that offered.

The Great Southern & Western Railway published around 1900 a substantial 240 page hardback guide *The Sunny Side of Ireland*. Its opening pages, shown on the next page, started with the Dublin-Holyhead crossing labelled 'the Swan's Back' as explained in the text. The first spread focussed on the City of Dublin's Royal Mail steamers. The LNWR and its *Cambria* came afterwards.

Across the "Swan's Back," from England to Ireland

ACROSS the "Swan's Back," as the Vikings called the Irish Sea, from Holyhead to Kingstown, there runs the finest line of Channel Steamers on our coasts. The passage may be made in two hours and three-quarters, and with calm, clear weather is like an excursion across the expanse of a Canadian lake. In the twilight of golden autumnal evenings, or the silvery dawn of spring mornings, before the hills of Wales drop beneath the sky-line, already the mountains of Wicklow lift up their heads in welcome. The entrance to Dublin harbour has been often compared to the Bay of Naples, the little brown moor beyond Howth Head stretches out before us, and the bold promontory of Bray, with Slieve Coolan—or, as it is usually known, the "Sugar Loaf"—and the highlands in the background, frame a picture of beauty rare. The City of Dublin Steam Packet Company has provided a new rapid service between the two countries. The magnificent twin screw steamers, "Ulster," "Leinster," "Munster," and "Connaught," so-called after the four provinces of Erin, sail twice each way daily with mails

DRAWING ROOM.   ROYAL MAIL STEAMER.   DINING ROOM.
SMOKING ROOM.   KINGSTOWN LANDING STAGE.

---

12   THE SUNNY SIDE OF IRELAND.

and passengers, running at a speed upwards of twenty-four knots an hour. These vessels are flush-decked, lighted throughout with electricity, and are fitted up in the most modern manner. For the convenience of passengers remaining on board the Night Mail Packet after arrival at Kingstown, a special train leaves the Pier each morning in connection with the different railway services into the interior of Ireland. The steamers leave Holyhead on the arrival of the 7.15 a.m. and 8.45 p.m. Mail-trains from London; on Sundays, on the arrival of the 10.45 a.m. train from Crewe, and the 8.45 p.m. from London, by the London and North-Western Railway's route. The Express steamers for the North Wall, Dublin, leave Holyhead on weekdays

ACROSS THE "SWAN'S BACK."   13

only on the arrival of the 9.30 a.m. and 10.15 p.m. from Euston. There is an extra service on Saturdays to meet train leaving Euston 4.10 p.m., the steamer arriving at North Wall 2.0 a.m. (Sunday). A favourite route of reaching Ireland is by the City of Dublin Steam Packet Company's line of vessels sailing from Liverpool every evening, except Sundays. These vessels run in connection with the Midland, Great Northern, Great Central, Lancashire and Yorkshire, and Cheshire Railways. They make the passage under eight hours, and are roomy and comfortable boats. Further information, and full details as to time, fares and routes, will be found in the ordinary Time Tables and Guides.

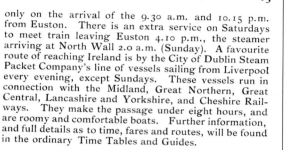

L. & N.W. S.S. "CAMBRIA."
(North Wall and Holyhead Route.)

---

12   THE SUNNY SIDE OF IRELAND.

and passengers, running at a speed upwards of twenty-four knots an hour. These vessels are flush-decked, lighted throughout with electricity, and are fitted up in the most modern manner. For the convenience of passengers remaining on board the Night Mail Packet after arrival at Kingstown, a special train leaves the Pier each morning in connection with the different railway services into the interior of Ireland. The steamers leave Holyhead on the arrival of the 7.15 a.m. and 8.45 p.m. Mail-trains from London; on Sundays, on the arrival of the 10.45 a.m. train from Crewe, and the 8.45 p.m. from London, by the London and North-Western Railway's route. The Express steamers for the North Wall, Dublin, leave Holyhead on weekdays

L. & N.W. S.S. "CAMBRIA."
(North Wall and Holyhead Route.)

The GS&WR guide featured some nice folding maps, provided as so often is the case by John Bartholomew in Edinburgh. The map shows the Irish railway system with the GS&WR system in bold. It does not show all the Irish Sea ferry services. Both Portpatrick-Donaghadee and Larne-Stranraer are shown but there is no Belfast-Liverpool service, nothing from Londonderry and nothing across the St Georges Channel. Omitting Fishguard is understandable, the harbour there did not open until 1906. This accounts for the lack of Rosslare (at Ballygeary on this map) and its rail link to Waterford which opened in 1906. A regular Waterford-Milford Haven service was working beforehand and its omission probably comes from the GS&WR's interest in funnelling traffic via Holyhead as the map emphasizes. Only Holyhead on the British mainland is in bold.

At Holyhead, the harbour facilities grew to a monumental scale. Construction of a breakwater over two kilometres in length showed that. The lions gracing the entrance to the Britannia Bridge had the same effect. This monumental arch was on the Admiralty Pier at Salt Island, Holyhead and was opened by King William IV in 1821. That pre-dated the railway and reflected the days of the Admiralty packets. The mail service did not leave this location until over four years after the 28 November 1920 take-over by the LNWR when their berths adjacent to the railway station were used. This improved the service since the tracks to the Admiralty Pier had required a change of locomotive for the last few hundred yards.

By 1956, the use of the Admiralty Pier and the City of Dublin Steam Packet for *Irish Mail* passengers was fading in the memory. Instead the enterprise seemed a thoroughly rail based business, indeed a British Railways-based business.

An attractive collectable would be one example of the named train leaflet issued by the London Midland Region. These are in a series with different titles and issued for each timetable season. There was probably upwards of a decade's worth although in the 1960s, the railway lost interest in promoting individually named trains. These folders had the train's timetable, a page of history and an attractive strip map of the route.

The timetable did reveal why to some companies (even to the present) the difference between Dun Laoghaire and a central Dublin terminal was important. Although only six miles apart, the timetable for the transfer from train to ship and thence the journey into town added more than an hour to the journey, which was quite an element when the crossing took $2\frac{3}{4}$ hours. Swings and roundabouts for as time passed, car drivers could be very thankful not to be disembarking in central Dublin.

The strip map from inside the summer 1956 *Irish Mail* brochure is adjacent. The leaflet is for the day service which at the time ran in the summer season only, perhaps the night service was not felt appropriate for the strip map style of publication?

Rather more of a challenge to track down (such that we cannot show it) would be an LMS version which existed as a substantial booklet. This was one of a series for their main routes. Entitled *The Track of the Irish Mail* editions from 1928 and 1947 written by Edmund Vale are known.

Over many years handbills for day trips to Ireland were published by the railway. This might seem reasonable enough in the vicinity of the British ports but such facilities were advertised over a huge spread of Great Britain. British Railways Eastern Region issued such ephemera. The example shown overleaf is for London Midland Region London passengers and used the night *Irish Mail's* services. It certainly was a long day of $33\frac{3}{4}$ hours for a stay of just under twelve hours in Dublin. That the facilities were advertised for so long suggests there was a market.

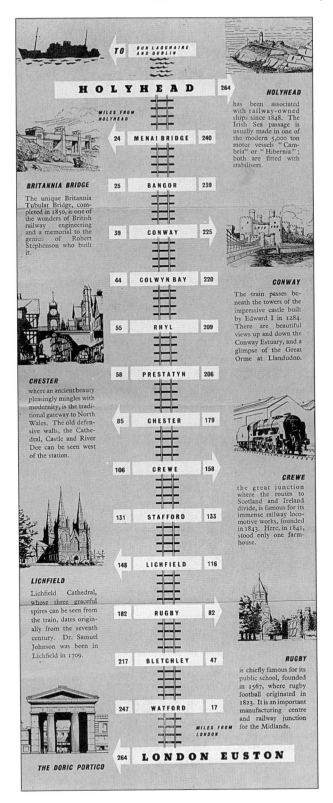

HOLYHEAD

HOLYHEAD has been associated with railway-owned ships since 1848. The Irish Sea passage is usually made in one of the modern 5,000 ton motor vessels "Cambria" or "Hibernia"; both are fitted with stabilisers.

BRITANNIA BRIDGE
The unique Britannia Tubular Bridge, completed in 1850, is one of the wonders of British railway engineering and a memorial to the genius of Robert Stephenson who built it.

CONWAY
The train passes beneath the towers of the impressive castle built by Edward I in 1284. There are beautiful views up and down the Conway Estuary, and a glimpse of the Great Orme at Llandudno.

CHESTER where an ancient beauty pleasingly mingles with modernity, is the traditional gateway to North Wales. The old defensive walls, the Cathedral, Castle and River Dee can be seen west of the station.

CREWE the great junction where the routes to Scotland and Ireland divide, is famous for its immense railway locomotive works, founded in 1843. Here, in 1841, stood only one farmhouse.

LICHFIELD
Lichfield Cathedral, whose three graceful spires can be seen from the train, dates originally from the seventh century. Dr. Samuel Johnson was born in Lichfield in 1709.

RUGBY is chiefly famous for its public school, founded in 1567, where rugby football originated in 1823. It is an important manufacturing centre and railway junction for the Midlands.

TO DUN LAOGHAIRE AND DUBLIN

MILES FROM HOLYHEAD			*MILES FROM LONDON*
	HOLYHEAD	264	
24	MENAI BRIDGE	240	
25	BANGOR	239	
39	CONWAY	225	
44	COLWYN BAY	220	
55	RHYL	209	
58	PRESTATYN	206	
85	CHESTER	179	
106	CREWE	158	
131	STAFFORD	133	
148	LICHFIELD	116	
182	RUGBY	82	
217	BLETCHLEY	47	
247	WATFORD	17	
264	LONDON EUSTON		

THE DORIC PORTICO

Spend a Day in Eire!!

LONG DAY TRIPS
FROM
EUSTON
TO
DUBLIN
Via HOLYHEAD & DUN LAOGHAIRE

EACH FRIDAY NIGHT
11th JANUARY until 10th MAY 1957
(EXCEPT GOOD FRIDAY 19th APRIL)

SECOND CLASS THROUGHOUT

s.　　　d.
70/6

SALOON ON STEAMER 20/- EXTRA

CHILDREN under three years of age, free ; three years and under fourteen, half-fares.

OUTWARD	RETURN SAME SATURDAY NIGHT
EUSTON　..　..　..dep. 8 45 pm	DUBLIN (Westland Row) ..dep. 7 10 pm
	DUN LAOGHAIRE (Steamer)　　„　8 40
HOLYHEAD　..　..arr. 2 35 Morn am (Sat.)	HOLYHEAD ..　..　..arr. 11 55
HOLYHEAD (Steamer) ..dep. 3 25　„	Sat. night/Sun. Morn.
DUN LAOGHAIRE　..arr. 6 40　„	HOLYHEAD ..　..　..dep. 1 10 am
DUBLIN (Westland Row) arr. 7 23　„	EUSTON ..　..　..arr. 6 30 Morn.) (Sun.

The tickets are valid on the date for which issued and by the services specified.

TICKETS CAN BE OBTAINED IN ADVANCE AT STATIONS AND OFFICIAL RAILWAY AGENTS, OR FROM BRITISH RAILWAYS TOWN OFFICES.

SEE OVER

BRITISH RAILWAYS

PLEASE RETAIN THIS BILL FOR REFERENCE

(BRITISH RAILWAYS)

DAY TRIPS
TO
NORTH WALES and CHESTER

MONDAYS
JULY : 1st, 8th and 15th. AUGUST : 26th
SEPTEMBER : 2th and 9th

TUESDAYS
JULY : 2th, 9th and 16th. AUGUST : 20th and 27th
SEPTEMBER : 3th and 10th

WEDNESDAYS
JULY : 3rd and 10th. AUGUST : 21st and 28th
SEPTEMBER : 4th and 11th

THURSDAYS
JULY : 4th and 11th. AUGUST : 22th, and 29th
SEPTEMBER : 5th and 12th

Leaving DUBLIN (Westland Row) at 8.00 a.m.
Leaving DUN LAOGHAIRE at 9.15 a.m.
Returning from HOLYHEAD by the 2.30 p.m. sailing
same day or 3.25 a.m. sailing following morning

Tickets will be issued to the following stations :—

STATION		From Westland Row	From Dun Laoghaire
		2nd Class Through-out	2nd Class Through-out
		s. d.	s. d.
Holyhead	... ...	26 6	24 6
Bangor	... ...	30 6	28 6
Colwyn Bay	... ...	33 6	32 0
Rhyl	... ...	35 0	33 6
Chester	... ...	39 6	38 0

SALOON ON BOAT EXTRA

Children under three years of age, free : three years and under fourteen, half-fare.

FREE LUGGAGE ALLOWANCE

Passengers holding day or half-day Excursion Tickets are not allowed to take any luggage except small handbags, luncheon baskets or other small articles intended for the passenger's use during the day.

CONDITIONS OF ISSUE

These tickets are issued subject to the British Transport Commission's published Regulations and Conditions applicable to British Railways exhibited at their stations or obtainable free of charge at station booking offices.

PASSPORTS, TRAVEL PERMITS or STEAMER RESERVATION TICKETS ARE NOT REQUIRED

Tickets in advance and all information can be obtained at Stations and Agencies, or from
G. B. GRAY, General Agent, 15 Westmoreland Street, Dublin.

Eric N. Webb & Co., Dublin'—E3590

This handbill from 1957 is a piece of British Railways publicity issued for Eire-originating traffic. It caters for the day excursionist in the reverse direction and covering summer weekdays it provides for a slightly less wearisome jaunt than the previous piece, taking in the North Wales resorts. Although in the main the style is that of a typical railway handbill of the time, a Dublin printer is used. Other Dublin-issued BR handbills are known

This facility in mirror image is shown in the 1959 handbill here. There are two significant additions. The appearance of the route logo which thence had a currency of some years and the cover image of one of the 1949 *Cambria/Hibernia* motor vessels. This image was used quite often on such handbills.

Viewing of Irish Mail Vessels

You are cordially invited to visit the Irish Mail vessels at Holyhead Harbour. They are available for inspection between 10.00 am to 12.00 noon and between 2.30 pm & 7.00 pm. Mondays to Fridays 1st June to 11th September (5.0 pm on 4th and 11th September) except 24th and 31st July, 6th, 7th, 10th, 13th, 14th, 20th, 21st and 28th August and the mornings of 30th June 1st, 7th, 8th, 14th, 15th, 27th, and 28th July. The charge for admission to the vessels is 1/- for Adults and 6d. Children.

Tea may also be obtained on board up to 5.30 pm (4.30 pm on 4th and 11th September) at 2/6 per head.

The reverse of the handbill detailed yet another facility. For the visitor who simply wanted to visit the ship just for its own sake, anyone at Holyhead was 'cordially invited to visit the *Irish Mail* vessels at Holyhead Harbour'. This cost 1*s* (the author would love to see a ticket for this) and Tea could be obtained on board. The viewing hours were a little bit like hospital. Two hours in the morning, four-and-a-half hours in the afternoon. What unhurried utilisation of assets that so discretely sought to maximise the return on capital!

Our visit to Heysham revealed the fine artwork that a British Railways carriage print could produce of an Irish Sea ferry. Another example of Claude Buckle's work, which also comes from 1957, shows the 1949 Harland & Wolff *Cambria*. The weather portrayed is perhaps a bit more realistic than many representations.

The same steamer or its sister appeared on many issues of the route's own timetable of which this Winter 1957 example is typical. At least two versions of the drawing were used. The route logo (already seen previously) is in evidence. It seems to have been used between at least 1957–1961.

In 1962, the logo had gone but there was signed artwork by Maddox. Then through 1963-1966 covering the transition to the corporate image, there were some staggeringly dull examples of publicity. Two different 'designs' of cover appeared, both equally boring. Opposite is the first, it had a nameless map for a cover. The next design did not even have that.

The interior was slightly better and included a page of commentary about the 'Ships of the Narrow Seas' which

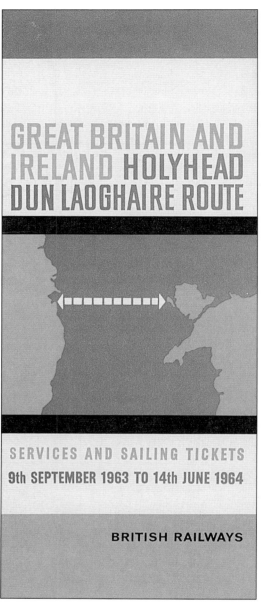

GREAT BRITAIN AND IRELAND HOLYHEAD DUN LAOGHAIRE ROUTE

SERVICES AND SAILING TICKETS
9th SEPTEMBER 1963 TO 14th JUNE 1964

BRITISH RAILWAYS

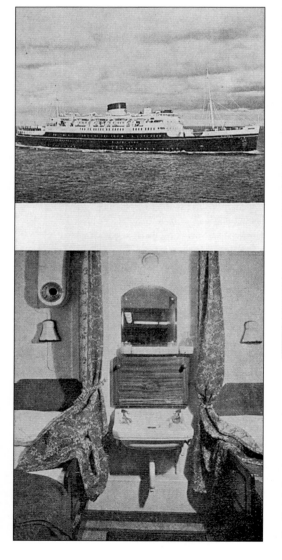

added that the SS *Princess Maud* would help out *Cambria* and *Hibernia* at peak times. There were also monochrome illustrations including cabin shots.

Princess Maud went right back to 1934 and the Denny yard which delivered her for service at Stranraer. Since 1947 Holyhead had been her home but she was used as an Irish Sea relief. She was withdrawn in 1965 and a career as a Greek-owned ferry followed.

Princess Maud's demise was brought about by the arrival of a new car ferry at Holyhead in 1965 – the first new vessel to be so used at the port. In concept she had some parallels to *Caledonian Princess* and was, like that vessel, steam turbine-powered. Her builders, however, were Tyneside's Hawthorn Leslie.

The absolutely uninspiring name arose because a new London Midland Region ferry manager had come from Atlantic Steam Navigation and was wedded to the ....*Ferry* series. It did not work and there never was a *Holyhead Ferry 2*. Somehow the name of the ship chimed in well with the uninspiring leaflets and was a huge difference to what had been happening at Stranraer.

With her close sister, *Dover*, they formed the last two new steamships BR bought. The Irish Sea vessel went for scrap in 1981.

The drawing below showing *Holyhead Ferry 1* is signed 'Wolstenholme': A.N. Wolstenholme, who did a range of work for both British Railways and Ian Allan, the railway enthusiast publisher. It is taken from a significant publication whose cover is illustrated as no.15 of the colour section. The Holyhead route leaflet may have been uninspiring that summer but this thirty-four-page booklet was a bit more impressive. It was reasonably well illustrated in monochrome and featured the three routes that the London Midland Region had an interest in: two mail services from Heysham and Holyhead and the new car ferry at the latter port. Never did the name of the new car ferry actually feature in the brochure!

Evidently this was the first issue of this publication. The initially summer-only car ferry service mushroomed leading to the borrowing of other BR car ferries later in the 1960s. I doubt very many editions of this publication appeared. I have no others and by 1970 the first of a great many Sealink A4 brochures covering the entire country had appeared rendering a regional issue superflous.

Before that it is clear that the various Irish Sea rail-owned car ferry routes had started to share publicity using a 'British Rail Irish Seaways' brand and producing a unified brochure in 1967-1969. In size and style the LMR 1965 offering is looking backwards and not forwards. There is no use of the double arrow and its origins are best seen in a series of *Irish Cross Channel Timetables* booklets that had existed since 1954 and which will be shown later.

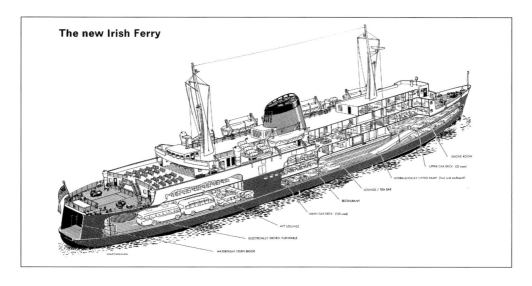

The new Irish Ferry

Amongst the series of British Rail-issued official postcards first discussed at Heysham, T.S.S. *Holyhead Ferry 1* featured. The card is likely to be from the 1965-1969 period. The corporate image rail blue is featured, the ship is from 1965 and carried no other colours, yet there is mention of British Railways London Midland Region on the reverse with no mention of Sealink. In 1976 the vessel was re-named *Earl Leofric*.

ENJOY THE ADVANTAGES OF A DAYLIGHT SEA CROSSING

the daytime

IRISH MAIL

British Rail Shipping Services

Earlier in the chapter reference was made to the *Irish Mail* named train brochure and that it was identified with the day sailings in 1956. Some ten years later these daytime passenger-only sailings still existed in summer. I doubt that the named train leaflet had survived through to 1966. However a little folder targetted at these sailings did exist all to itself – and had done so since at least 1964 and probably some time before. Such tiny collectables (four sides only) appeal for their very specialised nature and through their flimsiness, the two combining to reduce their survival rate. The *Cambria/Hibernia* pair had by now gained corporate image colours and a double arrow which they kept till withdrawal in 1975.

The mid-1960s propensity for some LMR marketing gaffes continued with this pair of ships. There are two significant brochures, one the author knows of only by repute. This latter comes from 1965 and was called 'Cruise across to Ireland with British Rail' and had pictures of the

Avalon and the *Lord Warden*, both then strangers to the area. The furore meant that the brochure was withdrawn. In the 1970s those ships did make it to Irish Sea services.

Compounding this the 1965-1966 Heysham-Belfast brochure whose layout is clearly shared with the Holyhead issues has an aerial picture inside of one of the Holyhead *Hibernia/Cambria* pair and not the expected Duke.

Mid-1960s British Railways in the throes of both mammoth contraction and yet also significant expansion (car ferries being a key such area) is obviously capable of throwing up interesting and unusual takes on our subject. Alongside Freightliner, Sealink and Inter City, BR in the late 1960s threw up another highly successful brand name. This was Motorail, an operation that lasted until privatisation destroyed marginal cost operations after 1995.

Motorail had existed as Car-Carrying (or Car-Sleeper) services since 1955. It had not taken very long to associate such services with key railway-owned ferry crossings.

Once a car ferry was in operation at Holyhead it made sense to run a linking Car Carrying service. An equivalent to Fishguard for Rosslare started in 1965. Holyhead's started in 1966. Stranraer never saw Motorail although trainloads of new cars for delivery were handled there.

Accordingly Motorail publicity is relevant to our story especially route specific leaflets such as that shown.

London—Holyhead or Dun Laoghaire

Car-Carrying Services 1966

Get there sooner — take your car by train

British Rail

Car-Carrying Services

Through bookings to Ireland were very much part of the object so the Irish terminal is named on the cover above – although the service also functioned for a North Wales holiday market. Inside the ship link was made more explicit. A vignette of the 1949 motorship duo appeared underneath the lines referring to the new car ferry – which these were not. The two ships are shown tied up at the head of the inner harbour at Holyhead (both images are overleaf). That location can easily be worked out from the accompanying map of the loading point. The map shows how the car ferry left (at that time) from a quite different location near the mouth of the harbour and requiring drivers to move their cars about a mile.

Another area of BR's activity which saw growth after thorough exploration of a blind alley was containerised freight. As with the service at Heysham, worthwhile publicity for the Holyhead-Dublin freight operations existed (overleaf).

Loading Points

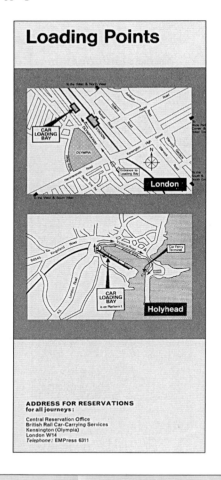

London

Holyhead

ADDRESS FOR RESERVATIONS
for all journeys:

Central Reservation Office
British Rail Car-Carrying Services
Kensington (Olympia)
London W14
Telephone: EMPress 6311

Stay in bed and go places

This overnight train can add as much as two days extra to your holiday. You leave home one evening, and arrive at your destination early the next morning. Your car goes on the same train and you travel the most comfortable way that exists — in bed.

Your Sleeper is just like a bedroom with everything where you want it. Wall-to-wall carpets, bedside lights and plenty of hot water are just a few of the comforts that help to make your journey completely relaxing.

In the morning the Sleeper attendant will bring you morning tea, or coffee, and biscuits.

On arrival your car is carefully unloaded. And if you are going on to Ireland, you drive straight to the ship.

A British Rail car ferry at Holyhead will carry you and your car to Dun Laoghaire in just a few hours. These modern ships give you a carefree crossing during which you can enjoy the well-stocked bars, full meal and snack services, and very comfortable cabins.

50,000 BRITISH RAILWAYS CONTAINERS AVAILABLE FOR YOUR TRAFFIC

THESE ARE THE PRINCIPAL TYPES

British Railways door-to-door containers, which are principally of the ten different types shown below, are specially designed to meet the extremely varied needs of the industrial and trading communities.

There are many uses to which containers can be put and from time to time new types are introduced or existing types adapted to keep up to date with the constantly changing requirements of transport users.

SMALL WHEELED Type SW
This covered unit was introduced to meet the needs of traders who wish to forward goods in small lots without recourse to elaborate packing. The wheels give easy movement in firm's premises and railway depots.
Length 5' 5½'; Width 3' 1'; Height 4' 3½'; Capacity: *Cubic feet 70; Weight 1 ton maximum;* Tare 5½ cwt.

DEMOUNTABLE TANK
British Railways have an arrangement whereby tank equipment for the conveyance of liquids in bulk can be constructed to traders' requirements and hired out to them on advantageous terms. Special features such as glass, stainless steel or plastic linings can be incorporated in the design.

MEDIUM COVERED Type A
Suitable for confectionery, groceries, boots and shoes, wireless apparatus, textiles, etc.
Approximate interior dimensions: Length 7' 0' to 7' 4'; Width 6' 9' to 6' 9'; Height to centre 6' 9' to 7' 3'; Capacity: Cubic feet 260-330; *Weight* 4 tons.

FURNITURE Type BK
Specially designed for furniture removals and new furniture. Fitted with interior slats for tying.
Approximate interior dimensions: Length 14' 10' to 15' 8'; Width 5' 6' to 6' 7'; Height to centre 5' 11' to 7' 4'; Capacity: Cubic feet 650-735; *Weight* 4 tons.

HIGHLY INSULATED Type AF
This container is designed for quick frozen foods and ice cream to be kept at very low temperatures. It has 9 inches of insulation all round. The usual method of refrigeration is by dry ice (CO_2).
Approximate interior dimensions: Length 5' 10'; Width 5' 4'; Height to centre 5' 2'; Capacity: Cubic feet 193; *Weight* 3 tons.

MEDIUM OPEN Type C
Caters for glazed ware, stoves, grates, ranges, heaters and small types of machinery, etc.
Approximate interior dimensions: Length 6' 11' to 7' 3'; Width 5' 11' to 6' 0'; Height to centre 2' 10' to 3' 6'; Capacity: Cubic feet 126-157; *Weight* 3 and 4 tons.

SMALL OPEN Type H
Cubic feet 46; *Weight* 2½ tons.

LARGE COVERED Types B & BD
Used for earthenware, tinware, enamelled ware, electrical equipment, etc., and for larger consignments of a similar variety of goods to those carried in the A type.
Approximate interior dimensions: Length 13' 5' to 15' 10'; Width 5' 10' to 6' 3'; Height to centre 6' 5' to 7' 3'; Capacity: Cubic feet 500-733; *Weight* 4 and 5 tons.

BK Type with special fittings
British Railways are willing to provide fittings in containers to suit particular flows of traffic. This is an example of a modified BK type container which has been equipped with rods to convey unpacked clothing. The interior dimensions are the same as for the BK Furniture Container described above.

LARGE INSULATED Type FM
These containers are completely insulated and extensively used for transporting frozen or chilled meat, and fresh produce such as eggs, butter and fruit requiring to be kept at moderately low temperatures.
Approximate interior dimensions: Length 14' 0'; Width 6' 6'; Height to centre 7' 1' to 7' 4'; Capacity: Cubic feet 587-632; *Weight* 4 tons.

LARGE OPEN Type D
For machinery, stoneware, castings, baths, asbestos sheets, slates, tiles, pipes, accumulators, motor engines, etc., and similar classes of goods to those carried in the C type.
Approximate interior dimensions: Length 12' 0' to 13' 9'; Width 6' 0' to 6' 3'; Height to centre 3' 0' to 3' 8'; Capacity: Cubic feet 215-300; *Weight* 4 tons.

NIGHTLY SAILINGS IN EACH DIRECTION VIA HOLYHEAD DUBLIN

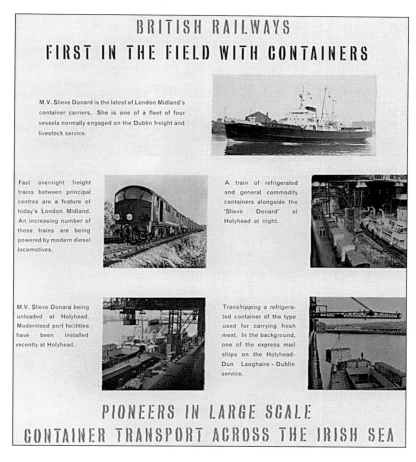

Artwork by Ronald Maddox has previously been mentioned, but not shown. Illustration 16 of the colour section is an example and such a piece of signed freight publicity is by no means unique – the most dramatic examples being commissions to Terence Cuneo for posters, but not I believe for Irish Sea material. There are other Maddox covers for the Holyhead-Dublin freight service.

Inside this leaflet (opposite) for 1962 the containers used were shown. Essentially this was inter-war technology, although BR had developed them to come in all sorts of shapes and sizes. The variety was well shown in the double page spread inside the leaflet.

Monochrome images were also used (above). That to the bottom right shows *Slieve Donard* berthed at Holyhead in the Inner Harbour. In the background either the *Cambria* or *Hibernia* is tied up in the berth shown in the Car-Carrying leaflet previously seen. The freight train is certainly a containerised express but is unlikely to be a Holyhead service. The engines are two infamous Metropolitan Vickers Type 2. Used for a short time in this fashion on a freight express between London and Glasgow called *The Condor*, they were a remarkable failure whose greatest claim to fame was an asymetrical Bo-Co wheel arrangement which has gained fame through the type's re-appearance in *Thomas the Tank Engine* stories.

The *Slieve Donard* was extremely relevant. She was a 1960 motorship from the Ailsa yard at Troon. Designed to carry livestock, containers or cars, she was deployed as a real car ferry at times, spending the summer of 1966 on the Fishguard-Rosslare route. This vessel could not carry all that many containers and as the livestock trade went over to lorries, her role diminuished leading to her sale in 1976.

The real need later in the 1960s was to accommodate the internationally acceptable ISO container. In 1968 two ships were specially designed with this aim in mind for service from Harwich: M.V.s *Sea Freightliner 1 & 2*.

On the Irish Sea routes, the first Freightliner to be carried went on the *Caledonian Princess* on 3 August 1966 in order to bring back to Britain twelve tons of Gallagher's cigarettes made in Ulster.

To provide a full Freightliner service out of Holyhead, two more ships based on the 1968 design were obtained in 1970. These were built at the Verolme Cork Dockyard near Cobh in Ireland.

It was intended that M.V. *Rhodri Mawr* and M.V. *Brian Boroime* would operate new services to Dublin North Wall and Belfast from Holyhead. Unfortunately their appearance more or less co-incided with the Britannia Bridge fire and for well over a year Heysham became the home port.

After this, the two ships became regulars at Holyhead on their intended duties until in December 1989 the privatised Sealink closed the freight routes and sold the vessels. *Rhodri Mawr* is pictured in front of *Brian Boroime* at Holyhead on 18 May 1986. The view is taken looking into the apex of the inner harbour as seen in the vignette previously and where the railway station was located and thus the berth of the *Irish Mail* steamers.

That mention of the Britannia Bridge fire is the key to the route's single most unsettling episode – it was not exactly a disaster as fortunately nobody was even hurt. The disturbance that the fire caused did lead to some very special publicity. The fire took place on 23 May 1970 and the bridge was out of use until 31 January 1972.

Between those times the literature had to cover for the move of the *Irish Mail* services to Heysham from 25 May 1970. Holyhead retained the car ferry and a special local rail service on Anglesey from a re-opened Llanfair PG. station was operated. Sadly, I have not yet found anything from the summer of 1970; these pieces presumably exist. The first cover shown is for the winter 1970/71 timetable. Whilst not of visual consequence, the document is of obvious note. Despite the Holyhead–Dublin cover everything inside revolved around a table for the night and peak day service routed via Heysham. The magic words *Irish Mail* were nowhere in sight. One small panel summarised the remaining car ferry sailings at Holyhead which, in the dead of winter, only operated in the Christmas holiday. How times change!

The same principles applied for the leaflet issued for the summer 1971 services. The cover expressed the hope that the bridge would re-open on 1 August 1971.

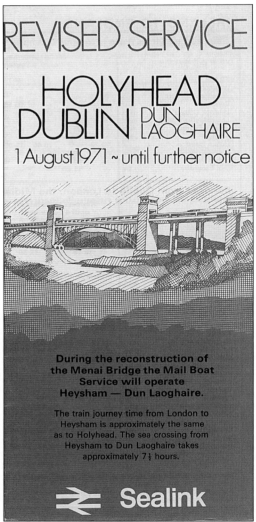

The bridge did not re-open in August 1971 and I cannot supply all the answers for this mystery leaflet (above left). The leaflet is for the full *Irish Mail* service (the names even re-appear inside) from Holyhead that never operated. Since BR must have had some notice that things were not working out, how and why this item was produced mystifies me. A clue comes in the print code where the date 11.11.70 indicates just how far in advance such items were ordered. I am pretty confident that the leaflet was never widely distributed.

Instead another leaflet on the principle previously enumerated appeared (above right). It had one significant addition. The cover could show artwork for the new bridge even including the new deck for road vehicles. That did not appear for some years. This artwork appears on another leaflet issued around November 1971 with a validity to 30 April 1972 which expressed the hope that the bridge would re-open the following January.

That happened and so the artwork made a triumphant re-appearance from 30 January 1972. This time everything worked out and the named services were back in the printed spotlight inside. As the mailship arrived at Holyhead from Dun Laoghaire it was greeted with snow on the ground and fireworks in the air.

Despite their peculiar circumstances and attendant covers, these leaflets were essentially members of a standard port series of Irish Sea route services that Sealink had now adopted. The map cover was current in the early 1970s, a view of a train/ship passenger interchange was in use from May 1972 and was duly used for that issue's Holyhead timetable.

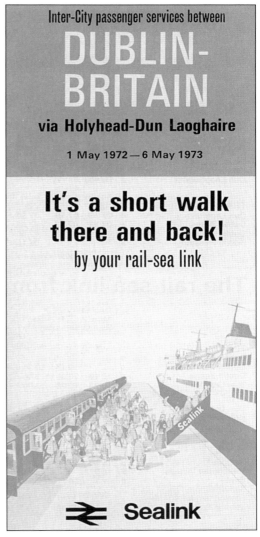

There was another run of literature affected by the bridge's closure. It is notable for one more item of artwork for the re-constructed bridge but this time omitting the road deck. The main timetable issued by the London Midland Region required substantial modification. Shipping services at two ports, their connecting trains and local trains along the North Wales coast were affected. A supplement was almost certainly issued in the summer of 1970 for the LMR 1970-1971 timetable which started on 4 May 1970. Others followed, the two the author has for 3 May 1971 and 3 January 1972 use this artwork. The one shown is wholly dedicated to the Britannia Bridge problem and evidently was produced over the winter of 1970-1971 (like the leaflet previously seen) when re-opening for August 1971 was anticipated.

SPECIAL SUPPLEMENT
to
Passenger Timetable
3 May 1971 to 30 April 1972
LONDON MIDLAND

Superseded by Alterations of 4/10/71
(Bridge not re-opened in August)

RECONSTRUCTION OF BRITANNIA BRIDGE (MENAI)

Continuation arrangements for the diversion of Irish services from Holyhead to Heysham—
including alterations to North Wales services

3 May to 31 July/1 August 1971
or until further notice

There followed thirteen years of stability and growth. In 1975, the two 1949 ships went, replaced for a year or so by stand-ins like the *Caledonian Princess*. There were to be no more all passenger ships and in 1977 another car ferry built for the route made its appearance.

The M.V. *St Columba* (below) came from the Danish yard of Aalborg Vaerft in 1977. She had a massive capacity of 2,400 people and a slab-sided profile to match. Internally substantial areas of the ship could be closed off to economise in the off season, She became a stalwart on the route into the mid-1990s. In that time five colour schemes were worn: Sealink rail blue; Sealink British Ferries, as seen in this view of her at Holyhead on 18 May 1986; Sealink Stena; Stena Sealink and Stena colours followed.

Along the way in 1991 she was renamed *Stena Hibernia*. Ever since her launch degrees of misfortune bugged her, including in January 1990 a major engine room fire off Anglesey.

An unusual item of Sealink ephemera was a 120 piece jigsaw issued of her in rail blue days.

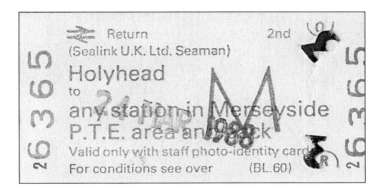

Every now and again in this book's view a sideways glance at tickets has been taken. In the Stranraer chapter an unusual yet relatively modern classic Edmondson card ticket was unearthed. Pure chance enables much the same theme to be seen for Holyhead operations.

The ticket is endorsed '(Sealink U.K. Ltd. Seaman)'. There is an explanation that what happened is that the former railway operations when privatised were required to recognise what had been railway staff travel concessions. This process was taking place just as the Edmondson card ticket was being withdrawn with the result that the combination of the facility with the ticket design is bound to be unusual.

This particular ticket was issued on 24 March 1988 and its validity to any station in the Merseyside PTE area would enable a large range of destinations to be covered.

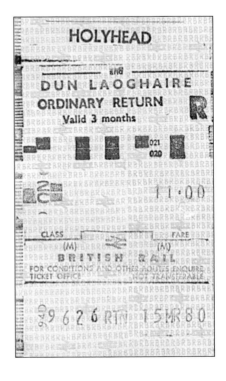

The next ticket does cover a conventional passenger's sea journey: in fact a crossing the author made on 15 March 1980. It is what you got if you turned up and wanted to go at the railway booking office at Holyhead. Being all one authority at the time, the result was just the same in terms of ticketing as if the author had asked for a ticket to Rhyl. In itself the ticket has no suggestion that it is for a sea voyage.

The ticket type is a bit offbeat being a pre-computerisation machine printed design. Technically called a 'Handiprinter', these were popular at middle-ranking London Midland Region stations for about twenty years. Fortunately the printing head was well inked on this example as the tickets could be almost illegible.

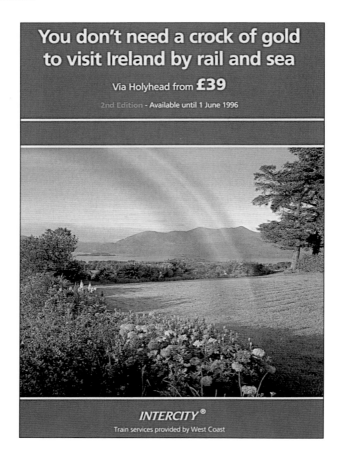

In bringing the story relatively up to date, it is possible to eyeball unusual material. Since 1984 the ferry operations at Holyhead have been independent of the railway and have gone through a further handful of image changes themselves. For a while the railway connections were stable but from the mid-1990s rail privatisation put paid to that.

At the turn of the millennium Virgin Trains were producing their own literature dealing with linking services across the Irish Sea through Holyhead. In the run up to privatisation BR created an organisation, a fully-fledged company called West Coast. This was given its own identity, privatised and promptly disappeared into the Virgin brand.

Throughout the later BR period both the railway and various forms of privatised Sealink had produced literature focussed on the rail-sea passenger, but for potential scarcity the small sequence of West Coast items with their blue/maroon colours must be noteworthy. This sixteen-side A5 brochure was well produced. Inside an artist offered views of the Menai Bridge, an Irish bar etc. By this date there were two ferry operators at Holyhead, Irish Ferries (ex B&I) and Stena. Colour images of their vessels including Stena's new High Speed Superferry were used.

All in all a notable future collectable and this 'Second Edition' was only valid for the three months from March–June 1996. The author has traced about six such leaflets issued between 1995 and 1997 after which Virgin red took over. The local train operators also produced Irish connectional literature and this, branded Regional Railways North West or North Western Trains, will be equally rare.

Mention of Irish Ferries/B&I requires an explanation about how the railway port that had seen off the City of Dublin company in 1920 was once again hosting an Irish-owned ferry company, indeed the one which had bought the old City of Dublin company.

Previous chapters have outlined something of the complexity of how an erstwhile Coast Lines company eventually in 1995 lost its identity in the Irish Ferries operation.

In the 1970s B&I operated Liverpool-Dublin and Swansea-Cork. At the time of this last year timetable shown above the routes were Holyhead-Dublin and Pembroke-Rosslare.

B&I had arrived at Holyhead with a daylight service to Dublin from 6 April 1982, but only after much antagonism from Sealink had been overcome.

The vessel on the cover of the 1994 brochure was the then flagship and when introduced in 1992 was the Irish Sea's largest passenger ferry at nearly 20,000 tons, though the much smaller *St Columba* had had a larger passenger certificate. Chartered from Stena Line in 1992, she dated from 1986, being built for the Danish State Railways. All pretence of the classic lines of the traditional packet steamer had totally gone. Her appearance made something like the *Caledonian Princess* seem puny yet in just two/three years her outline was itself totally overtaken by the fast ferry revolution where the demands of high speed stream-lining created something out of science fiction. This M.V. *Isle of Innisfree* was replaced by Irish Ferries in 1995 by a new-build M.V. *Isle of Innisfree* which, after a couple of years at Holyhead, left for the Pembroke route. This newer vessel has duly graced Irish Ferries brochure covers – see the end of the final chapter.

The sheer complexity of the dismemberment of the Sealink image may baffle. There are pundits who still cannot understand why such incredibly successful brands as Sealink and Intercity were discarded by new owners. Sea Containers had kept the Sealink brand as Sealink British Ferries. Stena went through Sealink Stena Line, Stena Sealink and Stena Line on the ships and the literature.

That's by the by. Aside from the image the major innovation by Stena has seen the advent of fast ferries. On the Irish Sea, Sea Containers had started the process at Stranraer. Stena initially bought the same technology: Incat Hobart-built catamarans. Their first route using the *Stena Sea Lynx* (under charter) was Holyhead-Dun Laoghaire opened on 16 July 1993. There were both A4 and A5 launch brochures using this cover. The 110-minute crossing time virtually halved the journey.

Since then Stena's Finnish-built High Speed Superferries have appeared on the brochures and eclipsed the much smaller Incat-built catamaran. That transition at Holyhead took place in 1996. It had been scheduled for 1995 but there were serious delays. The first four editions of the all routes A4 brochure that year gave the subject much space, and then the autumn edition (issue 5) had to accept a wholesale rewrite.

The Holyhead story can end with a 1995 contrast. This is a view of Greenore, a London & North Western-created railway town on the shores of Carlingford Lough which, between 1873 and 1951, looked to Holyhead as its ferry partner.

Far back in the twentieth century, it had been the setting for a little known tragedy comparable to the *Princess Victoria*. In foul weather on the night of 3 November 1916, the LNWR steamer *Connemara* left the port. She was at the mouth of Carlingford Lough when she collided with an unlit collier. All eighty-six people aboard were lost, indeed only one crew member of the collier survived to tell the tale.

Greenore's port survived the abandonment by the railway and in the 1990s was a flourishing freight and lorry port. Buried in the harbour complex the old London & North Western Railway hotel still bore a 'Hotel' sign.

This chapter has made much of LNWR official postcards. These featured Greenore: Alsop's postcard LNW325 has the title 'L&NW Bungalows, Greenore Golf Links'. The author has a memory from 1995 that he saw wooden bungalows at Greenore, little thinking that they were the product of LNWR enterprise although knowing that the hotel and its golf course were LNWR creations. The author does not have this card and Alsop only records two printings. Other LNWR Greenore and Carlingford Lough cards are more abundant.

Greenore stands as one of the oddest but still most characterful expressions of the relationship between British railway companies and Irish Sea shipping.

Six

South West Wales and the Great Western

The oldest regular ferry passage between South Wales and Ireland was the Waterford-Milford Haven mail route.

As the railway age dawned, the South Wales Railway proposed in 1845 a Gloucester-Fishguard route and a new harbour there. The Great Western Railway bought this company and opted for the less ambitious task of going to established Milford Haven. Their own operation of ships from that port commenced in 1872.

The early years of the twentieth century saw three new 'greenfield' ports developed for the Irish Sea traffic. The Midland Railway opened Heysham in 1904. Joint investment between the Great Western and the Great Southern & Western Railways saw the creation from 1894 of the Fishguard & Rosslare Harbours & Railway Company, a company still in existence albeit its public face is virtually non-existent. This opened the new harbours at Fishguard and fifty-four miles away at Rosslare which dominate this chapter.

This postcard view was mailed nearby in September 1906 and shows the railway station at Fishguard Harbour nearing completion, the view is looking inland towards London along an artificial shelf that had had to be created. The huge island platform on the right hand side is still recognisably present with the far face in use in 2001.

"Mauretania Special" Fishguard Station.

The complex opened in August 1906 after some two million tons of rock had been moved. This collotype Locomotive Publishing Company postcard is dated to about 1909 and shows the opposite end of the station. It is a scene full of Great Western paraphernalia like the parachute water tank, the lower quadrant semaphore signals and four engines, two each on two trains. Number 3402 is prominent and she was City class *Halifax* built late in 1908. The station was evidently attracting attention well after its opening day and that was because as the card's title suggests, the Great Western had perceived a glamorous use beyond the Irish bread and butter traffic: Fishguard ocean liner terminal. Cunard's first *Mauretania* connections began operating on 30 August 1909.

There are early cards covering the Irish traffic, one of Tuck's titles is 'The Fishguard Boat Express to Ireland'. This second example of a Locomotive Publishing Company card titled 'Cunard Special Leaving Fishguard' shows three interesting features. These are the use of the double-headed 4-4-0s to cope with the load, the brown liveried train giving an Edwardian date rather than the Great Western's conventional chocolate and cream, and the rock face which controlled the creation of the new complex whose buildings lie behind the signals to the right.

Looking forward nearly fifty years the opportunity is taken to narrate one rather special British Railways publication dealing with the Irish Sea traffic. The appearance of a nation-alised unitary authority interested in the trade, albeit without a monopoly, gave someone the idea of producing an entire *Irish Services Timetable*.

The Summer 1954 edition, whose cover is reproduced as illustration 17 of the colour section, is known to be the first edition. The map shows a total of fourteen routes and inside sixty-four pages were dedicated to the subject. Beyond the timetables there were adverts, a detailed list of the ships engaged in the trade, and pictures of the ships and the trains. Unfortunately the paper quality is not of the best in any of the issues so the illustrations I have had to set aside, even so one edition of this work needs to be on the must have list for those interested in Irish Sea shipping. It appears that such a splendid item was free.

BRIEF INFORMATION CONCERNING THE SHIPS CONNECTING WITH TRAIN SERVICES

All ships are fitted with the latest modern aids for safe navigation including radar.

The GLASGOW—LONDONDERRY service is conducted by the motor vessel "LAIRDSLOCH", a post-war vessel of 1,735 tons with very comfortable public rooms and sleeping accommodation in single and double berth cabins.

The GLASGOW—BELFAST service is operated by the two motor vessels "ROYAL SCOTSMAN" and "ROYAL ULSTERMAN", each of 3,250 tons. These modern ships have accommodation for 1,200 passengers with sleeping accommodation for a total of 314, mostly in single and two berth cabins. They have extremely comfortable and well appointed public rooms with ample seating in lounges and smoke rooms.

The GLASGOW—DUBLIN service is maintained during the Summer by the motor vessel "IRISH COAST". This ship of 3,800 tons, built in 1952 is fitted with stabilisers, and the passenger accommodation is of a very high standard. She carries a total of 1,200 passengers with sleeping accommodation for 380 in single and two berth cabins. The "IRISH COAST" acts as a relief vessel on four other routes during the Winter months. The "LAIRDSHILL" takes over the Glasgow—Dublin service in the Winter. She is a ship with a well earned reputation for comfortable travel.

The ARDROSSAN—BELFAST daylight service is operated by the 21 knots R.M.T.S. "LAIRDS ISLE" carrying 1,250 passengers on her four hour passage. This ship carries passengers only for whom there is ample deck space with roomy lounges, Dining Rooms, Smoke Rooms and Verandah Cafe.

On the STRANRAER—LARNE service there is only one regular ship, at present the S.S. "PRINCESS MARGARET", a vessel of some 2,550 tons. With sleeping accommodation for 157 passengers and the usual public rooms available to passengers, she is a compact and comfortable ship, ideally equipped for this short sea crossing.

The HEYSHAM—BELFAST service is at present operated by the "Duke" Class of Steamer, the "DUKE OF ARGYLL", "DUKE OF LANCASTER" and "DUKE OF ROTHESAY". They are each of approximately 3,800 tons and have sleeping accommodation for 384 passengers, mostly in single and double cabins. The public rooms are tastefully decorated and furnished.

The LIVERPOOL—BELFAST service is maintained by the motor ships "ULSTER PRINCE" of 4,300 tons and "ULSTER MONARCH" of 3,800 tons, both vessels reaching a high standard of comfort and luxury. Each has cabin accommodation for over 400 first class passengers, in addition to that for third class passengers. The dining rooms, lounges and smoke rooms are spacious and conveniently arranged.

On the LIVERPOOL—DUBLIN service are the motor vessels "LEINSTER" and "MUNSTER", both of 4,200 tons. These fine post-war vessels, both built for this service, with sleeping accommodation for 373 passengers, are tastefully decorated and furnished throughout. The public rooms consist of a general room, ladies retiring room, smoke room and bar, also a popular tea and snack bar. There is ample accommodation for the carriage of passengers' motor cars.

Between LIVERPOOL and CORK runs the S.S. "KENMARE", a comfortable steamer of 1,675 tons, carrying passengers, cargo and livestock. There are berths for 64 passengers and a good lounge and dining saloon.

The HOLYHEAD—DUN LAOGHAIRE service is normally maintained by the fine post-war motor vessels "CAMBRIA" and "HIBERNIA", also by the S.S. "PRINCESS MAUD" at busy periods. The two first named ships are luxuriously appointed for all passengers, and the lounges, smoke rooms, dining saloons and bar give an impression of an ocean liner in miniature. Both vessels have accommodation for 2,360 passengers with sleeping berth accommodation for 436, mostly in single and double private cabins. They are fitted with stabilisers and with a gross tonnage of practically 5,000 are among the largest cross channel vessels in the world.

The "PRINCESS MAUD" although a smaller vessel of nearly 3,000 tons, has sleeping accommodation for 202 passengers.

Passengers' motor cars are not conveyed by the Holyhead—Dun Laoghaire route but are carried by the direct Holyhead—Dublin North Wall route.

The FISHGUARD—ROSSLARE route has the "Saint" Class steamers, "ST. ANDREW", "ST. DAVID" and "ST. PATRICK" of varying tonnages of between 3,000 and 3,500. The accommodation on these vessels also varies slightly, but there are berths for some 345 passengers on the two first named and for 288 on the latter. The public rooms include the usual dining saloons, lounges, smoke rooms and bar, comfortable and well equipped. Each of these vessels carry over 30 motor cars.

The FISHGUARD—WATERFORD service is operated by the "GREAT WESTERN", one of the smaller of the British Railways' fleet. Of approximately 1,750 tons, she has sleeping accommodation for 86 and comfortable dining saloon and lounges.

The FISHGUARD—CORK route is operated by the M.V. "INNISFALLEN", a post-war vessel of some 3,700 tons, built to replace her predecessor lost by enemy action in 1940. Passenger accommodation is luxurious, consisting of single, double and de luxe cabins ; spacious lounges, smoke rooms, bars and a restaurant where the cuisine is of the highest standard. The vessel is fitted with DENNY-BROWN Stabilisers. Accommodation is available for over 30 motor cars.

This is the ship list from the Summer 1954 issue. A sequence similar to that employed by this book ensured that the Burns & Laird vessels came first and that Fishguard's BR steamers came last. The ownership of the vessels only became clear in each timetable entry.

The timetable did evolve a bit. The version of the cover shown (illustration 18 of the colour section) replaced the first in the summer of 1956 (on what was a twice-yearly issued publication).

By then an even more splendid colour fold out map had appeared in the inside back cover without which an issue of this period is not complete.

The timetables were full of information about the connecting named trains, about car shipping, and as CIE dieselised their trains before British Railways, it was their new diesel trains that appeared first.

The changes that did take place prior to the summer of 1963, which is the last issue the author has, were not on the whole revolutionary. The *Caledonian Princess* was hardly feted in this publication. A matter of interest to Fishguard did gain notable space in the Summer 1959 issue. Not only can the Fishguard-Waterford service be shown but the threat of its demise is covered.

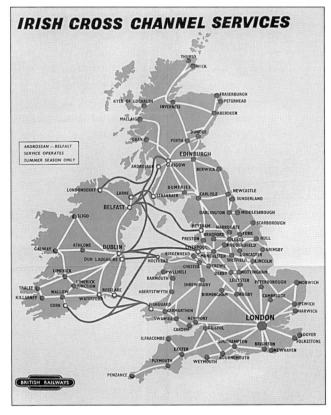

IRISH CROSS CHANNEL SERVICES

ARDROSSAN — BELFAST SERVICE OPERATES SUMMER SEASON ONLY

BRITISH RAILWAYS

FISHGUARD — WATERFORD
(BRITISH RAILWAYS)
MONDAYS, WEDNESDAYS AND FRIDAYS ONLY.

Bath Spa	depart B	4 25 pm
Birmingham Snow Hill	A	3 45 pm
Bristol Stapleton Road	A	5 06 pm
Bristol Temple Meads	A	5 00 pm
Cardiff General		6 46 pm
Cheltenham Spa Malvern Road	A	4 55 pm
Exeter St. Davids	B	2 42 pm
Gloucester Central	A	5 10 am
Hereford	A	4 25 pm
Llanelly		7 22 pm
London Paddington		3 45 pm
Neath General	H	7 15 pm
Newport (Mon.)		6 23 pm
Oxford		12 45 pm
Plymouth	B	1 10 pm
Reading General		2 38 pm
Salisbury	A	1 38 pm
Shrewsbury	A	3 05 pm
Swansea High Street		8 05 pm
Swindon	A	2 30 pm
Taunton	B	3 22 pm
Wolverhampton Low Level	F	2 35 pm
Worcester Foregate Street	E	3 20 pm
Fishguard Harbour	arrive	10 00 pm

| FISHGUARD HARBOUR | ... | ... | Vessel depart | 12 00 midnight |
| WATERFORD | ... | ... | arrive | 8G 00 am |

NOTES
A — via Cardiff.
B — via Bristol Temple Meads and Cardiff.
C — via Didcot, Swindon and Cardiff, On Fridays dep 1 11 pm, via Swindon and Cardiff.
E — via Hereford and Cardiff

F — via Birmingham Snow Hill and Cardiff.
G — Tuesdays, Thursdays and Saturdays.
H — via Swansea.
J — via Clarbeston Road.

WATERFORD — FISHGUARD
(BRITISH RAILWAYS)
TUESDAYS, THURSDAYS AND SATURDAYS ONLY

| WATERFORD | ... | ... | Vessel depart | 6 30 pm |
| FISHGUARD HARBOUR | ... | arrive | 2 00 am |

		Wednesdays and Fridays			Sundays	
Fishguard Harbour	depart	3 55 am	4 55 am	7 50 am	4 35 am	6 45 am
Bath Spa	arrive E	9 16 am	D 10 57 am	E 2 06 pm	E 10 37 am	E 2 10 pm
Birmingham New Street		D	11 22 am			D	3 46 pm
Birmingham Snow Hill	A	10 55 am		D 2 50 pm	A 11 25 am		
Bristol Stapleton Road	A	8 20 am	A 9 53 am	A 1 55 pm	A 9 47 am	A 1 26 pm
Bristol Temple Meads	A	8 31 am	A 10 00 am	A 1 43 pm	A 9 57 am	A 1 36 pm
Cardiff General		6 55 am	8 07 am		11 52 am		7 43 am
Cheltenham Spa Landsdown		D	10 18 am				
Cheltenham Spa St. James	E	9 56 am		A1 1 33 pm	E 11 51 am	A 2 15 pm
Exeter St. Davids	E	10 47 am	E 12 10 pm	A 3 30 pm	E 12 32 pm	C 5 01 pm
Gloucester Central		9 05 am	9 54 am	A 1 19 pm	11 36 am	A 1 45 pm
Hereford	A	9 06 am	A 10 00 am	2 10 pm	A 9 30 am	A 2 24 pm
Llanelly		5 30 am	6 24 am		10 02 am		6 04 am
London Paddington		10 40 am	11 45 am	3 10 pm	11 15 am	2 40 pm
Neath (General)	C	6 45 am	G 8 20 am		10 45 am	B 7 23 am	9 35 am
Newport (Mon.)		7 22 am		8 32 am	12 18 pm	8 08 am	11 19 am
Oxford			F 11 13 am	F 4 11 pm	A 1 36 pm	F 3 22 pm
Plymouth	E	12 45 pm	E 2 03 pm	E 5 15 pm	E 2 20 pm	E 6 40 pm
Reading General		9 51 am		10 57 am	2 24 pm	10 25 am	1 47 pm
Salisbury		E	12 27 pm	A 3 44 pm	A 1 11 pm	L 6 35 pm
Shrewsbury		AK	11 43 am	B 4 05 pm	A 1 20 pm	A 3 42 pm
Swansea High Street	C	6 15 am	C 7 25 am		10 25 am		6 30 am	9 10 am
Swindon			9 59 am	1 33 pm	A 11 47 am	12 48 pm
Taunton		E	9 56 am	E 11 29 am	2 38 pm	E 11 38 am	E 3 20 pm
Wolverhampton Low Level	A	11 12 am		D	3 48 pm	A 11 41 am	
Wolverhampton High Level			H 12 11 pm				H 5 21 pm
Worcester Foregate Street		A 9 56 am	E 10 51 am	A 3 02 pm	A 10 33 am	A 4 06 pm

NOTES
A — via Cardiff.
B — via Swansea High Street.
C — via Llanelly.
D — via Cardiff and Gloucester.
E — via Cardiff and Bristol Temple Meads.
F — via Swindon and Didcot.
G — via Llanelly. On Saturdays arrive 7 53 am.
H — via Cardiff, Gloucester and Birmingham New Street.
J — via Reading General.
K — On Fridays, 17th July to 14th August inclusive arrive 11 28 am.
L — via Cardiff, Bristol Temple Meads and Westbury.
T — Cheltenham Spa Malvern Road.

Customs Regulations page 70
Baggage Regulations pages 70, 71
Travel Documents page 70
Ticket Information pages 69, 70, 71

PASSENGER FARES TO AND FROM WATERFORD VIA FISHGUARD

STATION	ORDINARY				
	SINGLE		RETURN		
	1st Class	2nd Class rail 1st Class in ship		1st Class	2nd Class rail 1st Class in ship
Bath Spa	93/3	79/6		176/6	149/0
Birmingham Snow Hill	106/5	83/7		206/6	156/0
Bristol Temple Meads	90/9	77/10		171/6	145/8
Cardiff General	81/2	70/4		152/6	130/2
Cheltenham Spa Malvern Road	86/0	71/5		171/0	132/3
Exeter St. Davids	109/6	90/4		209/0	178/8
Fishguard Harbour	52/0		94/0		
Gloucester Central	85/11	71/4		170/10	132/1
Llanelly	67/6	62/4		125/0	114/8
London Paddington	112/10	90/9		224/8	164/4
Newport High Street	84/0	70/6		158/0	130/7
Oxford	106/3	83/6		201/0	159/1
Plymouth	122/6	99/0		235/0	188/0
Reading General	108/6	87/3		207/0	163/6
Swansea High Street	70/5	64/2		130/6	118/4
Wolverhampton Low Level	106/8	83/9		212/4	156/4

IMPORTANT NOTICE

British Railways have submitted proposals to the Transport Users' Consultative Committee for Wales and Monmouthshire to surrender the passenger certificate on the S.S. " Great Western " and to withdraw as from 29th June, 1959 the passenger facilities between Fishguard Harbour and Waterford, Adelphi Wharf.

At the time of going to press, these proposals were still under consideration by the Transport Users' Consultative Committee. In the event of the passenger service in question being withdrawn, attention is directed to the facilities available for passengers and accompanied motor car traffic via the Fishguard Harbour/Rosslare Harbour route.—for details see pages 42 to 45.

SAILING TICKETS

Sailing Tickets (see General Information) will be required for the following sailings :—
To Ireland | From Ireland
All sailings: Friday nights 17th July to 31st July | Saturdays nights, 1st, 8th, 15th 22nd and 29th August.
inclusive also Friday nights, 7th and 14th August.

SEAT RESERVATIONS

Seats are reserved on the following trains in connection with the sailings to and from Waterford. The seats are reservable from the starting points of the trains, at a charge of 2/- per seat, and passengers are requested to apply to the SEAT RESERVATION BUREAU AT THE COMMENCING STATION :—
To Ireland
From London Paddington ... 3 45 pm Mondays, Wednesdays and Fridays.
From Ireland
From Fishguard Harbour ... 3 55 am Wednesdays and Fridays.
4 35 am Sundays.
4 55 am Wednesdays and Fridays.
NOTES :— Passengers travelling from Ireland must apply to the Agent, British Railways, Rosslare Harbour, by 4 00 pm three days prior to the date of sailing.

RESERVATION OF CABINS AND BERTHS ON VESSELS (Saloon Class only).

Cabins and berths may be reserved in advance on application by letter (enclosing remittance) to the addresses shown, at the following charges additional to the First Class fares :—

First Class (Saloon)	£ s. d.	First Class (Saloon).	
Special Cabin with toilet only	6 6.	Special Cabin with toilet only	2 0 0
(one person)	2 0 0	(two persons)	
		Two berth Cabin (per berth)	13 0

APPLICATION FOR RESERVATION OF CABINS AND BERTHS. FORWARD AND RETURN JOURNEYS.

Applicants at present living in Great Britain apply to :—
The Commercial Officer, OR The Station & Quay Superintendent,
Central Enquiry Bureau, British Railways,
British Railways (Western Region), Fishguard Harbour.
Bishop's Bridge Road, Goodwick, S.O.
Paddington Station, Pembs.
London W.2.
Applicants at present living in Ireland apply to :—
The Agent, British Railways,
Adelphi Wharf,
Waterford,
Republic of Ireland.
Cancellation of Berths—See page 68.

EMBARKATION AT THE PORTS
At Fishguard Harbour :— Between 7 00 pm and 8 00 pm and after 9 30 pm
At Waterford Adelphi Wharf :— From 4 00 pm.

DISEMBARKATION AT THE PORTS
At Waterford Adelphi Wharf :— Until 9 00 am.
At Fishguard Harbour :— Until 7 45 am.

Customs Regulations page 70
Baggage Regulations pages 70, 71
Travel Documents page 70
Ticket Information pages 69, 70, 71

Withdrawals by British Railways had to go through a statutory procedure designed to generate paperwork. Surviving items from railway closures always gain interest but such items for the closing of a railway-owned shipping service are much less common. In addition to the timetable note, the explanatory handbill (bottom left) was published.

The Waterford service was not as important as the Rosslare route. It was the old time favourite: steamships had linked Waterford and Pembrokeshire since 1824. It went into a long decline and the passenger service was withdrawn in 1959 as intimated in the timetable. The livestock trade had been its mainstay and cargo sailings continued but the *Great Western* was withdrawn from the route at the end of 1966. Chartered vessels continued the route until 1977.

The mention of S.S. *Great Western* by name sparks comment. She was a 1934 vessel, which spent most of her life undertaking the service. There had been two *Great Western* predecessors (1867 and 1902). The earlier Brunel-designed paddleship, the 1837 *Great Western*, was never a Great Western Railway ship, unlike the three later vessels.

The *Irish Services Timetables* may have lasted a little bit longer than 1963 but before long it was replaced. One replacement would have been the *London Midland Region Car Ferry Handbook* seen earlier. Another is shown now.

It represents the integration (for a time) of Irish timetable information into the pattern set for BR's other foreign connections. Between 1948-1959, there was a one volume *Continental Handbook* to which the *Irish Services Timetables* can be seen in relation. Thereafter a series of national booklets often with very attractive signed covers were produced till 1974. Ireland already had its issue in 1959 and was not immediately affected by these developments.

WESTERN  REGION

PUBLIC NOTICE

The Western Region of British Railways announce that the Transport Users' Consultative Committee for Wales and Monmouthshire have agreed to the proposal for the complete withdrawal of passenger facilities from the s.s. "Great Western" operating between Fishguard and Waterford and on and from June 29th, 1959, passengers will cease to be conveyed by this route.

Facilities are available for passengers and accompanied motor car traffic via the Fishguard Harbour — Rosslare Harbour route. Bookings for passengers and motor cars already accepted on the Waterford service for June 29th and subsequent dates will be transferred to and honoured on the Fishguard — Rosslare sailings on the same dates. Passengers travelling via Rosslare will, if desired, be able to send their motor cars via Waterford at the accompanied motor car rate. Full details of sailing times and connecting train services on the latter route can be obtained from Stations and Enquiry Offices and Ticket Agencies.

J. R. HAMMOND,
General Manager.

By 1972 (towards the end of these booklets), this title existed (left). But when was it introduced? Having sifted various sources the author would now be surprised to find it prior to about 1970 and the overall weight of Sealink's advent. It is an eighty-six page volume but dominated by timetables far more than the *Irish Services Timetable* had been.

Focusing back on Fishguard: John S. Smith's artwork has been seen before. For a number of years through the 1950s and early 1960s, something similar to this handbill formed the basic document for promoting sailings through Fishguard. Its target was the rail passenger as the map cover makes evident, although information about shipping cars was provided. The three routes from Fishguard to Cork, Waterford and Rosslare are clear.

The document became a smaller leaflet around 1959 and the drawing covers favouring the 1947 *St Patrick* went soon after 1962. At least five different ship drawings were used and at times the 1947 *St David* was featured – a different hull window arrangement helps tell them apart. These two ships were to the Fishguard services what the 1949 *Hibernia* and *Cambria* were at Holyhead save that these were steam turbine vessels and their BR service only lasted till 1970-1971. The Cork service was not a BR route but involved the City of Cork company, which was a Coast Lines company about which more will be explained. This service occupied three out of this document's twelve pages.

A small sequence of what now appear very dated leaflets covers the package or 'all-in' holidays that could booked via the Fishguard route. The promoter has been encountered

BRITISH RAILWAYS

an tòstal
IRELAND AT HOME

DAY EXCURSION BOOKINGS
Monday, May 11th
Wednesdays, May 13th & 20th
TO

SOUTHERN IRELAND

(via FISHGUARD and ROSSLARE)

PADDINGTON ... ... depart 6 55 p.m.

TO	ARRIVAL TIMES	Return Fares		RETURN DEPARTURE TIMES
		Second Class Throughout	Second Class Rail and Saloon on Boat	
	a.m.	s d	s d	p.m.
ROSSLARE HARBOUR	5* 30	71/3	94/0	11† 15
WATERFORD NORTH	7* 12	81/9	102/3	9† 24
WEXFORD NORTH	7* 17	73/6	96/0	10† 5
CORK	10* 10	104/6	125/6	6†·30

PADDINGTON arrive 10.40‡ a.m.

Passengers for Waterford North and Cork proceed from Rosslare by rail at 6.15 a.m. and for Wexford North at 6.40 a.m.
*—Tuesday and Thursdays
‡—Wednesday and Fridays
†—Tuesday and Thursdays

Children under Three years of age, Free ; Three and under Fourteen years of age, Half-fare

TICKETS AT THE SAME FARES AS FROM PADDINGTON MAY ALSO BE OBTAINED AT THE FOLLOWING STATIONS:—

Westbourne Park, Acton Main Line, Ealing Broadway, West Ealing, Hanwell & Elthorne, Southall, Hayes & Harlington, West Drayton & Yiewsley, Uxbridge (Vine Street), Cowley, Staines West, Colnbrook, Iver, Langley, Slough, Windsor & Eton Central, Burnham (Bucks), Taplow, Maidenhead and Greenford and passengers may, with these tickets, travel by Ordinary Trains between these stations and Paddington in order to connect with the above Trains.

Notice as to Conditions.—These tickets are issued subject to the British Transport Commission's published Regulations and Conditions applicable to British Railways exhibited at their Stations or obtainable free of charge at station booking offices. Luggage allowances are as set out in these general notices.

Tickets can be obtained in advance at Booking Stations and Agencies

For details of excursion bookings to CORK on Tuesdays and Thursdays—See other side.

Further information will be supplied on application to Stations, Agencies, or to Mr. N. H. BRIANT, District Operating Superintendent, or Mr. E. FLAXMAN, Commercial Officer, Paddington Station, W.2 (Telephone: Paddington 7000, Extension "Enquiries": 8.0 a.m. to 10.0 p.m.).

Paddington Station, W.2.
April, 1959.

before with Manx material. I know of leaflets between 1959-1962 and assume there would be others. Covers used drawings and appear to vary but the theme of train, ship and coach is maintained. CIE the Irish Transport company provided the coach tour in Ireland and the CTAC or Creative Tourist Agents' Conference the marketing in the UK.

The phenomenon of the day excursion that was anything but has been encountered with other routes. This example for Fishguard services in the Spring of 1959 has a forty-four hour day for a trip from London to Cork. No mention was made in the handbill that this trip direct to Cork used a City of Cork vessel. The reverse of the handbill detailed thirty-nine hour days which reached Waterford, Wexford and Cork by train from Rosslare. Such long outings before the motorway or flying became popular were the way that many Irish families living in London kept in contact with their kin.

If the previous item probably picked up passengers with Irish relations, the next was more likely to appeal to the conventional tourist. This was a most ambitious forty hours worth whose key was through-the-night travel to and from Rosslare Harbour which left 15¾ hours for a trip on CIE's 'Radio' Train. Aside from the effort of going to Killarney for a Saturday with 2½ hours free time and then a fourteen mile jaunting car trip, it is those words 'Radio' Train which focus interest.

CIE not only dieselised before BR but introduced a train fitted with public address first, although BR followed with its own 'Radio' Trains. In CIE's case the first 'Radio' Trains (from 1949) were even steam-hauled.

The route from Rosslare to Waterford is still open but beyond to Mallow, most of which was Fishguard and Rosslare Railway & Harbours territory, closed in 1967.

WEEK-END EXCURSION TO

★ **KILLARNEY'S**
Lakes and Fells ★

in SEPTEMBER

Kindly Retain this Pamphlet for Reference.

— *from* —

LONDON (Paddington), READING (Gen.), WESTON-Super-MARE (Gen.), BRISTOL (Temple Meads & Stapleton Road), NEWPORT, CARDIFF (Gen.), BRIDGEND, PORT TALBOT (Gen.), NEATH (Gen.), SWANSEA (High St.), LLANELLY and CARMARTHEN.

(Via Fishguard and Rosslare).

Forward :
FRIDAY EVENING, 20th SEPTEMBER, 1963.

Returning :
SATURDAY EVENING, 21st SEPTEMBER, 1963.

Since accommodation is limited, you should make your reservations well in advance. Don't leave it too late.

 BRITISH RAILWAYS

ITINERARY IN IRELAND

Upon arrival at Rosslare, passengers join the C.I.E. Special " Radio " Train departing at 6 a.m.

The journey from Rosslare to Killarney runs through the historic city of Waterford, home of the famed glass industry of that name, skirts the South Irish Coast and proceeds through the pleasant valleys of the rivers Suir and Blackwater.

We pass Mount Melleray, site of widely-known Trappist Monastery, Lismore Castle, Irish seat of the Duke of Devonshire, and numerous other points of interest, before reaching Mallow, County Cork, an important centre of Ireland's agricultural industry.

A further brief journey takes us through, picturesque sylvan scenery and brings up the mountainous horizon which heralds Killarney, arriving at 10.0 a.m.

A programme of music will be provided throughout the journeys and will be interspersed with commentaries on places of interest en route.

Approximately 2½ hours free time is available for sightseeing, etc., before lunch, which can be arranged at a good class hotel from 12.30 p.m. to 1.30 p.m.

After lunch the tour of Killarney continues by jaunting car, a circular tour covering about 14 miles and embracing some of the finest scenery in an area renowned for its beauty. The tour passes through the Kenmare Estate, and along the wooded shore of the Lower Lake, visiting such world-famed places as Muckross Abbey, Dinis Cottage, the Meeting of the Waters, and Torc Waterfall.

The tour ends at about 4.0 p.m. and there is approximately 1 hour and 50 minutes free time before the return train departs Killarney at 5.50 p.m., arriving Rosslare Harbour at 9.40 p.m.

For details of MEAL ARRANGEMENTS and General Notes, etc., see page 4.

It was the influence of the motorist that at Fishguard, like all the other ports, came to dominate: such that whilst Fishguard in 2000 retained passenger trains, only two ship services each way have a rail connection. This far from full two-car diesel train dealt with all the rail-borne passengers for the day connection on 7 September 2000 with the railway now swamped by road facilties, much of which reflects a 1994 rebuild. In the 1950s small numbers of cars could be accommodated by craning onto the traditional steamers.

The change in emphasis seems to have been underway from 1959 by which year a parallel brochure to the standard route timetable already seen had appeared targetted at the motorist. Vehicles were 'conveyed on deck'. The example shown covered the winter sailings when one night sailing operated three days a week from each terminal. Fishguard's Irish services in the 1950s were not intense. Daylight sailings – summer only – only started to Rosslare with regularity in 1961.

The motorists' timetable (opposite, top) had extended to eight glossy sides in 1962, which itemised the thirty occasions when the extra 12.15 p.m. sailings from each terminal would operate.

Both reverse and front of this brochure carried the same artwork save that the reverse was signed Vincent Power. The leaflet might be thought to suggest that the era of deck cargo was over! Inside that phrase still appeared, it was only for the 1964 season that the *St David* was modified to allow cars to be driven on through a side door. Services were increased and cars carried in one year leapt from 11,000 to 20,000.

The car space was installed in what had been a cargo and mail hold and the side doors connected to a former cattle walkway tunnel on the Fishguard quayside whose dimensions were tight. Many many changes would be made to accommodate cars in coming years.

The 1960s became a decade of change reflected in the ships and the publicity neither of which settled down at Fishguard. Turbine steamers like *inter alia* the *Duke of Rothesay*, our old friend *Caledonian Princess* and the *Avalon* all appeared to grapple with the route.

It would take a lot of space to sort out the publicity for 1960s Fishguard services but an inkling of the experimentation that marked the period can be seen in 1965:

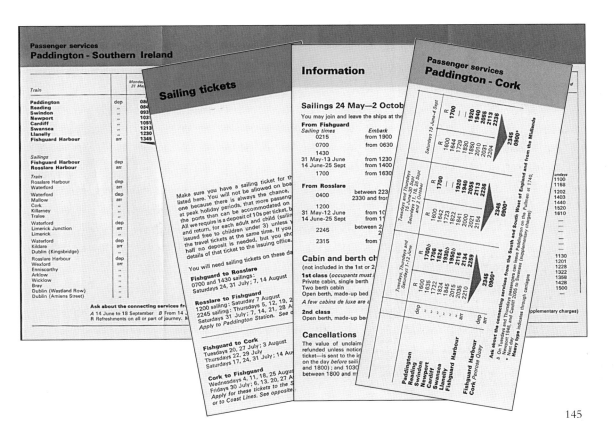

the first year of British Rail's corporate image. That year the pattern of a train-based and additionally a motorist's timetable continued. Each shared: a new size, evidently the one un-named designer, and a clever loose leaf insert form (previous page, lower) that enabled some documents to be shared: like a fold out map of Southern Ireland.

The cover, shown as illustration 19 in the colour section, is the train-based timetable. The leprechaun in different pose appeared on each timetable. The diesel engine, which was a Western-class diesel-hydraulic, was only on the train-based timetable. Where the cover shown had 'British Rail Shipping Services', its mate for the motorist proclaimed 'British Rail Western Region'.

In the summer of 1965 Fishguard enjoyed a welter of rail connections compared with the paucity of 2000. The local train service into Fishguard, using Fishguard and Goodwick Station, had just closed in 1964. That summer Fishguard Harbour's trains arrived at 0135 for the traditional 0215 night sailing, 0600 – a new overnight sleeper from Paddington, 1328 and 1345 providing in effect two trains from Paddington for the core daytime sailing, 1625, 2154 and 2236. The two last trains were connecting with the *Innisfallen* direct to Cork. Otherwise the trains connected with a summer maximum of four crossings to Rosslare.

The new London-Irish Car Carrier

Two days can be added to your southern Ireland motoring holiday if you use the new car-carrying service which is being introduced on 18 June.
Leaving London shortly before midnight, this overnight service will see car and passengers disembarked at Rosslare shortly after 10 o'clock next morning, all set for an early start.
Similarly, on the return, by sailing on the noon steamer, you will be back in London by late evening. The inclusive charge automatically reserves a compartment on the train (rugs and pillows are provided for the night journey) for a car party of up to four adults.

Times and dates
From London

Train		Ship	
Kensington (Olympia) dep 2355		Fishguard	dep 0700
Fishguard	arr 0445	Rosslare	arr 1015

On Friday nights—18 June to 9 July; and Sunday to Friday nights 11 July to 24 September.

To London

Ship		Train	
Rosslare	dep 1200	Fishguard	dep 1700
Fishguard	arr 1515	Kensington (Olympia) arr 2155	

On Saturday afternoons—19 June to 10 July; and Monday to Saturday afternoons 12 July to 25 September.

Baggage trailers, caravans, dormobiles or vehicles over 6' 3" high cannot be taken on this service.

Loading times
For the journey to Ireland cars must be at the Kensington Olympia Station (Russell Road) one hour before the departure of the train. On the return journey cars should be at Rosslare between 1000 and 1100 for the mid-day sailing.

Refreshments
Breakfasts, lunches and light refreshments are served on board the ship. There are no refreshment facilities on the train, but packed light meals for the journey to London can be obtained on board before disembarking.

Business was booming and there was another brand new train service into Fishguard. The sleeper had left Paddington at 2335 and went via Swindon and Gloucester. Meanwhile from the car carrier or Motorail terminal at Kensington Olympia a 2355 *London-Irish Car Carrier* had set out for Fishguard which it went to direct arriving at 0445 to unload for the 0600 sailing. From the 1965 motorists' timetable, the insert for this new service is reproduced. Note that this journey was not in a sleeper but a reserved compartment per carload of passengers was provided.

As at Holyhead a tranche of Motorail literature produced for this service is there to be found. Fishguard is 260 miles from London and before the M4 it was a terrible drive and it is still quite an undertaking. For some time the Motorail service flourished and adopted the redundant Fishguard and Goodwick station as its terminal. The summer of 1980 was the last year Motorail connections were offered.

Rosslare Harbour was a fascinating if not strange place. Although *St David* had a drive on facility in 1965, the ship's berth was not accessible to vehicles. The harbour comprised a breakwater against whose inside face the ships berthed. A

Rosslare Harbour
Early evening at Rosslare harbour with car ferry "Duke of Lancaster" berthed at the ramp after her journey from Fishguard. The whole scene is given a busy look with ro/ro traffic taking up every inch of space and the 18.30 hrs. train departure starting its journey to Limerick.

rail only bridge connected the harbour to the mainland and getting cars onto the mainland had seen them being craned onto rail wagons for a short journey.

This layout is clear in this mid 1970s view. The bridge had been widened for 1965 and a roadway squeezed in to a linkspan. Yet another ship was then on the service. The former Heysham *Duke of Lancaster*, now a rear door car ferry succeeded the *Caledonian Princess* for a while.

In the foreground is the station of Rosslare Harbour Mainland ex-Ballygeary. The sequence of events here is very complicated but worth summary: did any other ferry terminal go through so many changes?

Interest in the area started in 1864 when the Waterford & Wexford Railway was authorised. All it had managed to open by 1882 was a line from Wexford to 'Greenore Point' which had been intended as a branch of the original project. Greenore Point was effectively Rosslare Harbour. In 1889 money ran out and the line closed.

In 1894 the moribund Waterford & Wexford was taken over by the new Fishguard and Rosslare concern. Services to Rosslare re-opened in 1895. Another eleven years passed before the major harbour investment was finished and Rosslare Harbour Pier opened in 1906.

There were now stations at Rosslare Strand and then at Kilrane, which had been the original Rosslare Harbour station which was re-named in 1906 and closed in 1970. The rest of the tale occupied a mile and a quarter.

The train in the picture is just entering Ballygeary or Rosslare Harbour Mainland. This station opened in 1970 when Kilrane closed. As Ballygeary, it was open for less than a year when its temporary wooden platforms where replaced by something more permanent. The name change from Ballygeary to Rosslare Harbour Mainland took place in 1977 and the station was closed when another station was opened sixteen chains nearer the pier in 1989.

This was known as Rosslare Harbour until 1996 when it was re-named Rosslare Europort. Beyond Rosslare Strand, this is the only station now open.

Only now do we get to the pier which had in its first form opened in 1882 as Rosslare Pier. Until 1895 only special traffic was handled. That station was replaced by another one further out to sea in 1906. This was termed Rosslare Harbour between 1906 and 1977 when it became Rosslare Harbour Pier and then was closed in 1989.

Handling cars explains many of the later changes. When the viaduct was singled it became necessary to propel trains out onto the pier and the run round operations took place at Ballygeary/Rosslare Harbour Mainland. Ballygeary was also where the sidings and loading bank were located for handling the cars from the pier prior to 1965. Rosslare Harbour gained a second car ferry berth in 1979 by which time there were non-Sealink sailings to France to handle as well.

The source of this image has its own ephemeral interest. Just as the British Railway regional magazines had once covered shipping interests prior to 1963, so the Sealink organisation created its own house magazine. This appears to have been a quarterly publication which had reached issue forty by September 1983. The previous picture was the reverse cover of the May 1978 issue, the cover of that magazine being shown above.

That May 1978 issue contained further Fishguard interest. A story was illustrated with this image of the T.S.S. *Lord Warden*. This was a 1952 Denny-built car ferry for the Dover services. In the 1970s she appeared at various times at Holyhead and in 1978 added yet another name to the miscellany of vessels that worked from Fishguard. This time the task was an innovative summer daily service to Dun Laoghaire and back as well as undertaking an extra return crossing to Rosslare. This old ship was sold in 1979 and the Dun Laoghaire sailings abandoned. I have never seen any route specific literature for that initiative; what there may be must be most uncommon. A Sealink Irish Holidays brochure for 1979 and a Sealink German language 1979 timetable included the schedule that was intended for the Fishguard-Dun Laoghaire's services second season. These sailings were cancelled and no mention of the service was in the main Sealink timetable that summer.

Meantime Fishguard's quest for adequate capacity in 1979 saw the charter of the 1974 M.V. *Stena Normandica*. In the event she stayed till 1990 gaining the name *St Brendan* in 1985.

The mixture of vessels employed at Fishguard offered a visual tell tale even in the Sealink days of rail-blue. Vessels like the *St David* owned by the Fishguard company rather than solely British Railways were allowed an FR logo on their funnels instead of the double arrow.

Some readers will realise that captioning publicity material can offer its own challenge. Its originators were under no necessity to caption the images they used. That is something of the fun in collecting this material: the detective work to identify what is in front of you.

This means there is the danger of making mistakes which is my excuse for some hesitancy in saying that on the right hand cover of the accompanying brochure (overleaf) is a view of Paddington Station (safe there I think) whilst the left hand image shows the T.S.S. *Avalon* in the harbour at Fishguard. As someone who has only been to Fishguard once and not been out in the harbour which is surely how this picture was taken (from a small boat?), I am a bit wary of making a mistake.

Rail/Sea Services to BRITAIN via Rosslare–Fishguard
2 October 1978 to 13 May 1979

Rail/Sea Services to IRELAND via Fishguard–Rosslare
2 October 1978 to 13 May 1979

Inter-City ⇌ Sealink   Inter-City ⇌ Sealink

Nor is the ship's name legible despite some work with a magnifying glass and the brochure makes no mention of which ship was in use on the route. Images of *Avalon* can require careful interpretation as her stern area was heavily rebuilt when she became a car ferry in 1975 immediately prior to being sent for service at Fishguard. When new in 1963 she had been a passenger only packet for service from Harwich to the Hook of Holland. Additionally she undertook cruise duties in succession to the *Duke of Lancaster* whose activities in that field have been noted at Heysham. Once replaced in 1979 by the *Stena Normandica* she was soon redundant in the Sealink fleet.

This timetable must have been about the last issued during *Avalon's* Fishguard presence. At Heysham and Holyhead we have seen examples of larger 'standard' Sealink rail/ferry route timetables. Those seem to have been replaced by A7 folders like this in 1978. This series itself seems to have existed until 1980 for each Irish Sea route. Various other colour illustrations were used.

The matter of small A7 timetable folders or cards can take off in other directions. During the standard BR corporate image era, one in a huge series of railway-based A7 card timetables was issued for London-Dublin. Later, first Intercity West Coast and then Virgin have issued A7 timetable cards for services to Dublin/ Dun Laoghaire in their otherwise standard series.

The era of corporate image was collapsing under the Thatcherite governments of the 1980s and Sealink's 1984 sale to Sea Containers ushered in many quickfire changes in publicity, routes and ships.

At the tail end of the Sealink BR owned era from 1982 a brochure covering train and ship services via Holyhead and Fishguard came into being. In 1984, its inherited BR-designed artwork was slightly modified and the title 'Quick Guide to Ireland' adopted. Train connected services and car ferry information were combined.

During 1985 this title and route combination was used with new Sealink British Ferries artwork and their 'sleeve ring' symbol. This era only lasted until 1990 before the Stena takeover and makes all Sealink British Ferries items inherently noteworthy.

From what are a considerable number of these transitional pieces, we highlight the summer 1986 edition of the Quick Guide. Its cover showed the Holyhead route's *St Columba* in her new colours. Inside there were references and images of Fishguard's refurbished *St Brendan*, the erstwhile *Stena Normandica*.

Extracts, displayed overleaf, offered a further nuance to the competitive situation. For a short while Sealink British Ferries and B&I co-ordinated their Irish Sea sailings and so the latter's sailings were added. The timetable block from the leaflet shows this and an image of B&I's *Leinster*. The co-ordination was particularly marked at Fishguard where the sailings were jointly operated following B&I's abandonment in January 1986 of Pembroke Dock sailings.

A final item of note from the leaflet is the image of and information about the Supabus services. That was a 1980s brand by which National Express and CIE jointly promoted coach services to Ireland.

The coach's rather bulbous front design is the distinctive trademark of Dutch manufacturer Bova. Barely legible on the image is the vehicle owner's name on the front door. I only recognised the National London script by tracing the registration number A665 EMY in a fleetlist. This was one of ten toilet-fitted Bova Futura coaches delivered in 1984 to National Travel (London) Ltd. It was even named *Tempest*, which can just be seen above the indicators. The Supabus livery was only carried by a few vehicles in the fleet, two only in 1986. Those were sisters of the one shown which by then was in Thomas Cook colours.

This was a top notch vehicle for a small but top notch company which could trace its antecedents back to the 1840s but was about to face privatisation via absorption into the London Country group in 1987. Thus does one leaflet unpack so many themes.

TIMETABLES

HOLYHEAD ➡ DUN LAOGHAIRE	
operated by Sealink British Ferries	
Time	**Days/Dates of operation**
0315	Daily
1445	Daily
Crossing approx. 3½ hours	
Check in 45 mins	

DUN LAOGHAIRE ➡ HOLYHEAD	
operated by Sealink British Ferries	
Time	**Days/Dates of operation**
0845	Daily
2045	Daily
Crossing approx. 3½ hours	
Check in 45 mins	

HOLYHEAD ➡ DUBLIN	
operated by B+I Line	
Time	**Days/Dates of operation**
0530	Daily 13 June to 7 September
1715	Daily
Crossing approx. 3½ hours	
Check in 1.00 hour	

DUBLIN ➡ HOLYHEAD	
operated by B+I Line	
Time	**Days/Dates of operation**
1145	Daily
2300	Daily 12 June to 6 September
Crossing approx. 3½ hours	
Check in 1.00 hour	

FISHGUARD ➡ ROSSLARE The Southern Seaway	
operated jointly by Sealink British Ferries and B+I Line	
Time	**Days/Dates of operation**
0315	Daily
0600	Daily 23 May to 15 September
1500	Daily
1745	Thursdays to Sundays 10 July to 14 September
Crossing approx. 3½ hours	
Check in 45 mins	

ROSSLARE ➡ FISHGUARD The Southern Seaway	
operated jointly by Sealink British Ferries and B+I Line	
Time	**Days/Dates of operation**
0900	Daily
1200	Thursdays to Sundays 10 July to 14 September
2140	Daily
2355	Daily 22 May to 14 September
Crossing approx. 3½ hours	
Check in 45 mins	

LIVERPOOL ➡ DUBLIN	
operated by B+I Line	
Time	**Days/Dates of operation**
2215	Daily
Crossing approx. 8 hrs 45 mins	
Check in 1.00 hour	

DUBLIN ➡ LIVERPOOL	
operated by B+I Line	
Time	**Days/Dates of operation**
0900	Daily 13 June to 7 September
2300	Daily until 11 June and from 7 September
Crossing approx. 7 hrs 45 mins day 8 hrs 45 mins night	
Check in 1.00 hour	

In the fluidity of recent times, the adoption of high-speed ferry technology has been one consistent feature. Fishguard's turn came eleven months after Holyhead's conversion.

Holyhead's *Stena Sea Lynx* was moved to Fishguard to start the new service. The high-speed crossing allowed a maximum of five return sailings in the peak season. The brochure as a Stena Sealink item retained the Sea Containers era inspired 'sleeve ring' symbol. It is an A5 folder dedicated to the new route (above). There was a similiar one third A4 sized item (my example coming in an envelope glued to the standard A4 Stena Sealink 1994 brochure). 1994's two Irish Sea high-speed Stena Sealink services also had their own A4 brochure.

To keep the Holyhead service going the slightly different Incat *Stena Sea Lynx II* took up service there from 7 June 1994. The A4 brochure detailed this and illustrated both ships.

Co-operation between the railway-owned steamers and Coast Lines (and its predecessor/successor companies) regarding the St George's Channel routes went back a long way. Already this chapter has shown 1950s BR handbills in which the Cork route from Fishguard appeared fully integrated into BR's sales pitch, yet the route was run by a financially independent operator.

The Cork-South West Wales service had been operated by the City of Cork Steam Packet Company since 1875 although its antecedents go back to 1856 and a service between Cork and Milford Haven which the GWR bought in 1872 only to sell to the company three years later.

Fishguard's opening in 1906 naturally took the Cork service there, although in years to come the sub-theme of non-railway owned companies seeking to work out of Milford Haven or Swansea to Southern Irish ports would run and run.

Racing though earlier Cork history, the company joined Coast Lines in 1918 who made it a subsidiary of B&I in 1936. The sale of that company to the Irish Government in 1965 paved the way for Irish policy to compete with the British Railways-owned Fishguard crossings.

That was not the case in 1960 when traditional arrangements held sway. 'The *Innisfallen* Way' was a marketing term used both by the City of Cork and British Railways publicity. It highlighted the name associated with ships on the run from 1896.

There were five generations of *Innisfallen*. The leaflet and this coloured postcard (with its classic nightime pose) focus on the 1948 motorship. That was a standard Coast Lines design, its 1930 predecessor had been bombed to destruction at Liverpool in 1940 (the Fishguard run being then suspended). The 1903 version had been lost to the Germans in 1918. The ship offered an overnight service, which meant each port being served three days a week.

M. V. "Innisfallen"   Fishguard–Cork Service.

That sort of operation was leisurely and the car-mad swinging sixties brought radical change. In November 1968 B&I left Fishguard and sold the twenty-year-old *Innisfallen*. The next May a new car-carrying *Innisfallen* opened a Cork-Swansea service. For the lengthy route, machinery to achieve a very creditable 24 knots was installed. She was then the fastest car ferry in Northern Europe.

There then followed ten years of B&I leaflets in which one publication covered their twin car ferry routes Liverpool-Dublin and Swansea-Cork.

This decade of stability ended with this leaflet (right) and its 'Pembroke (Swansea)-Cork' descriptor on the cover for the 1979 season. That May, Swansea was abandoned by B&I in favour of a newly developed terminal at Pembroke Dock.

To go with the new service there was a new ferry the *Connacht*. The leaflet gave her plenty of attention including this cut away view. Other goodies within the leaflet were a CIE M class Leyland Leopard coach with its odd, to UK eyes, CIE-built body. M41 of 1971 did the honours whilst an even older CIE A class diesel engine number 100 was featured, both in colour. Number 100 my foot, there was no such loco. The photo was printed in the leaflet back to front, the engine was actually 001, the very first A class delivered from Metropolitan Vickers in Manchester in 1955.

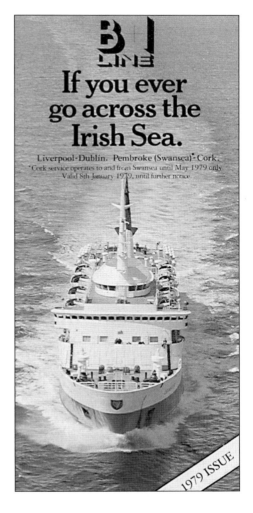

155

In 1980 B&I added services to Rosslare from Pembroke Dock but a succession of troubles dogged their services. Cork was abandoned in 1983 after *Connacht* was replaced by a revived *Innisfallen*, which was actually the renamed *Leinster* of the 1979 leaflet's cover.

The difficulties continued and led to the B&I/Sealink pool at Fishguard in 1985 leaving Pembroke Dock quiet.

B&I had another decade of life before it but after 1991 it was a component of what is now Irish Ferries, which itself had entered the private sector in 1987.

The turn of 1987-1988 saw B&I back at Pembroke Dock with their Rosslare sailings. That operation has continued to the millennium.

Some impressive vessels have followed. The 1970-built chartered *Munster* (not the B&I vessel of 1968) was on the Rosslare sailings in the early 1990s and appeared on the publicity. She was succeeded in 1992 by the near 20,000 ton *Isle of Innisfree*, a massive vessel whose form dominated a number of leaflets like this 1993 timetable (below, left). She was chartered from Stena having started life in 1986 as a DSB Danish State Railways ferry. The 1992 leaflets showed her first in her earlier livery and later in the B&I colours.

Over the next couple of years the B&I literature moved more and more to the Irish Ferries camp until...

On 1 January 1995 as suggested by this leaflet (below, right) a new roll on/roll off company appeared on the former B&I routes and with it a new ferry. The 1995 *Isle of Innisfree* was built for Irish Ferries in Holland. Initially used from Dun Laoghaire, in 1997 she shifted to Rosslare. Have there not been references to Irish Ferries before 1995?

Yes: the catch being that the B&I routes to Britain had till then escaped the Irish Ferries brand despite being so owned. They were the Irish Sea routes that the leaflet referred to.

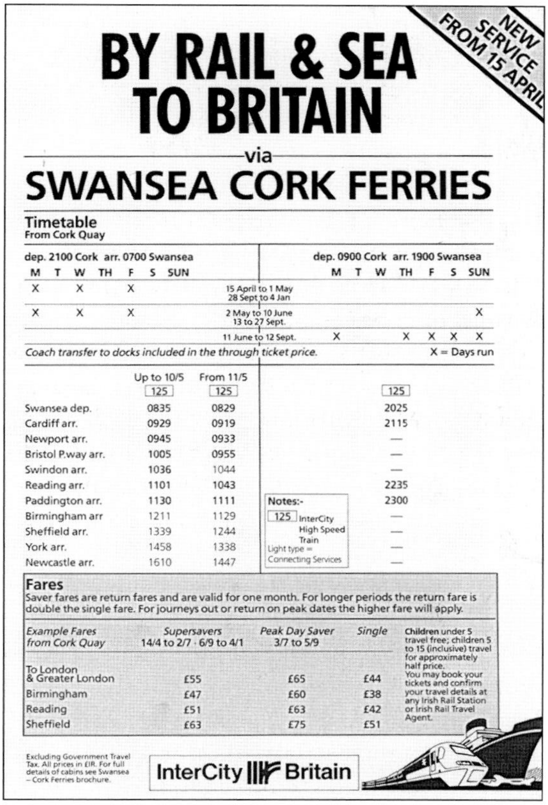

BY RAIL & SEA TO BRITAIN

NEW SERVICE FROM 15 APRIL

— via —

SWANSEA CORK FERRIES

Timetable
From Cork Quay

dep. 2100 Cork arr. 0700 Swansea									dep. 0900 Cork arr. 1900 Swansea						
M	T	W	TH	F	S	SUN			M	T	W	TH	F	S	SUN
X	X	X					15 April to 1 May 28 Sept to 4 Jan								
X	X	X				X	2 May to 10 June 13 to 27 Sept.								
							11 June to 12 Sept.	X		X	X	X	X		
Coach transfer to docks included in the through ticket price.													X = Days run		

	Up to 10/5 [125]	From 11/5 [125]		[125]
Swansea dep.	0835	0829		2025
Cardiff arr.	0929	0919		2115
Newport arr.	0945	0933		—
Bristol P.way arr.	1005	0955		—
Swindon arr.	1036	1044		—
Reading arr.	1101	1043		2235
Paddington arr.	1130	1111	Notes:-	2300
Birmingham arr	1211	1129	[125] InterCity High Speed Train	—
Sheffield arr.	1339	1244	Light type = Connecting Services	—
York arr.	1458	1338		—
Newcastle arr.	1610	1447		—

Fares
Saver fares are return fares and are valid for one month. For longer periods the return fare is double the single fare. For journeys out or return on peak dates the higher fare will apply.

Example Fares from Cork Quay	*Supersavers* 14/4 to 2/7 · 6/9 to 4/1	*Peak Day Saver* 3/7 to 5/9	*Single*	Children under 5 travel free; children 5 to 15 (inclusive) travel for approximately half price. You may book your tickets and confirm your travel details at any Irish Rail Station or Irish Rail Travel Agent.
To London & Greater London	£55	£65	£44	
Birmingham	£47	£60	£38	
Reading	£51	£63	£42	
Sheffield	£63	£75	£51	

Excluding Government Travel Tax. All prices in £IR. For full details of cabins see Swansea – Cork Ferries brochure.

InterCity Britain

Irish Ferries' other routes which have not been detailed were from Rosslare or Cork to French ports direct and so do not involve the Irish Sea. Their origins go back to 1973 when a new ferry named the *St Patrick* opened their Rosslare-Le Havre route.

Since 1995 the new *Isle of Innisfree* has appeared on a wide range of Irish Ferries items amongst which there can be little doubt that this flimsy two side A4 sheet is a collectable for the future.

The politicians and folk of both Swansea and Cork did not appreciate losing their ferry links. B&I pulled out in 1979 and in 1987 Swansea Cork Ferries re-opened the route. Since then a fascinating saga has developed, whose full representation publicity wise would be an interesting file's worth. The author has only a handful of items though this one stands for the first season. The company was jointly owned by the local authorities of West Glamorgan, Cork (city and county) and Kerry! The service was started with a chartered Polish ship renamed the *Celtic Pride*.

British Railways were prepared to connect with the ferries whether they ran from Pembroke or Swansea. A train from Pembroke Dock at 0125 was even laid on. It did not last long. The item shown above is a BR-produced, two side, A4 handbill providing the Swansea ship's timetable and its rail connections and key through fares. The New Service slogan is of note but no information about the ship was given. The side shown provided the from Ireland services and showed the IE (Irish Railways) logo, BR's own double arrow only appearing on the reverse side with the from Britain sailings.

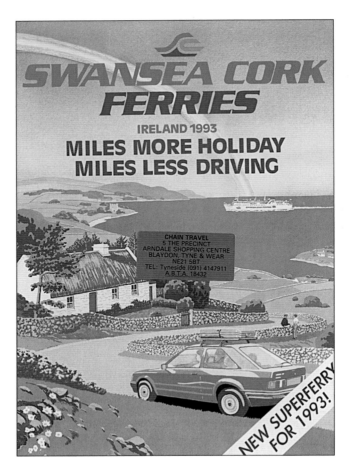

There were no sailings in 1989. Services resumed the next year followed by major changes in 1993, the year of the brochure cover shown. That year the Greek company Strintzis Lines bought the operation and introduced the 1972 Japanese-built *Superferry*. An artwork cover reproduced her and a Ford Escort with a thatched Irish cottage. Inside, there were photos of the ship.

Swansea Cork's interest has been maintained, since, as the author concluded writing this volume, a new arrival in 2001 was a ship named the *City of Cork* to run the service. She is none other than the erstwhile *St Patrick II* well known to Irish operations after 1982 when she operated Irish Ferries' French routes. At the time of publication, it was learnt that in 2002 the erstwhile *Superferry* would replace *City of Cork* on this route in 2002.

Our voyage is almost complete, the phrase *City of Cork* is redolent of the traditions and interests of Irish Sea shipping.

It would be possible to continue beyond Swansea. Mediterranean interests had been present on South Wales-Irish services before. In the mid-1970s Seaspeed Ferries of Limassol in Cyprus had worked from Barry Docks to Dublin and Cork. This was a commercial vehicle route and the author rates his chances of finding any publicity for that operation from only just over a quarter of a century ago as rather slim. Another attempt at the same route came in 1983 from Welsh-Irish Ferries and should promise further rare gems.

Appendix

Unit Load/Truck Freight Only Ferry Operators in the Irish Sea

Operator	Route	1971	1998
Anglo-Irish Transport	Preston-Londonderry	x	
Anglo-Irish Transport	Preston-Warrenpoint	x	
Atlantic Steam Navigation	Ardrossan-Larne	x	
Atlantic Steam Navigation	Preston-Belfast	x	
Atlantic Steam Navigation	Preston-Drogheda	x	
Atlantic Steam Navigation	Preston-Dublin	x	
Atlantic Steam Navigation	Preston-Larne	x	
B&I	Liverpool-Dublin	x	
B&I	Weston Point-Dublin	x	
Belfast Freight Ferries	Heysham-Belfast		x
Belfast Steamship Company	Liverpool-Belfast	x	
Bristol Steam Navigation	Bristol-Dublin	x	
British Railways	Fishguard-Waterford	x	
British Railways	Heysham-Belfast	x	
British Railways	Heysham-Dublin	x	
British Railways	Holyhead-Dublin	x	
Burns Laird	Ardrossan-Belfast	x	
Cawoods Container	Garston-Belfast	x	
Greenore Ferry Services	Preston-Greenore	x	
Greenore Ferry Services	Sharpness-Greenore	x	
Irish Sea Ferries	Garston-Warrenpoint	x	
Isle of Man Steam Packet	Heysham-Douglas		x
Merchant Ferries	Heysham-Dublin		x
Merchant Ferries	Liverpool Dublin		x
P&O European Ferries	Ardrossan-Larne		x
P&O European Ferries	Cairnryan-Larne		x
P&O European Ferries	Fleetwood-Larne		x
P&O European Ferries	Liverpool-Dublin		x
P&O European Ferries	Rosslare-Cherbourg		x
Palgrave Murphy (Shipping)	Dublin-Antwerp	x	
Palgrave Murphy (Shipping)	Dublin-Le Havre	x	
Palgrave Murphy (Shipping)	Dublin-Liverpool	x	
Palgrave Murphy (Shipping)	Dublin-Rotterdam	x	
Ronagency (Shipping) Ltd	Glasson Dock-Castletown	x	
Ronagency (Shipping) Ltd	Glasson Dock-Strangford	x	
Seatruck Ferries	Heysham-Warrenpoint		x

Sources for this Table
1971: *Container Ships*.   1998: *Ferries of the British Isles and Northern Europe*

Bibliography

A.B.C. Shipping Services (monthly), various publishers, various issues consulted.

Alsop, John: *The Official Railway Postcard Book*, John Alsop, Bedford, 1987.

Boot, Paul and Fenton, Roy: *Classic Coasters*, Ships in Focus Publications, Preston, 1997.

Carpenter, Reginald: *Container Ships*, Model and Allied Publications, Hemel Hempstead, 1971.

Christie's South Kensington: *British and Irish Travel Posters*, Christie's South Kensington, London, 1999 & 2000.

Clegg, W. Paul and Styring, John S.: *British Nationalised Shipping*, David and Charles, Newton Abbot, 1969.

Collard, Ian: *Coastal Shipping The Twilight Years*, Tempus, Stroud, 2000.

Cowshill, Miles: *Stranraer-Larne, The Car Ferry Era*, Ferry Publications, Narberth, 1997.

Cox, R. C. and Gould, M. H.: *Civil Engineering Heritage Ireland*, Thomas Telford Publications, London, 1998.

Cunningham, R. R.: *Portpatrick Through The Ages*, R. R. Cunningham, Portpatrick 1974.

Danielson, Richard: *The Isle of Man Steam Packet Volume 1*, Richard Danielson, Laxey, 1987.

Danielson, Richard and Hendy, John: *The Manxman Story*, T. Stephenson and Sons, Prescot, 1983.

Duckworth, C.L.D. and Langmuir, G.E.: *West Coast Steamers*, T. Stephenson and Sons, Prescot, 1966.

Goodwyn, A. M.: *Is this any way to run a shipping line?*, Manx Electric Railway Society, Lancaster, 1986.

Haresnape, Brian: *This is Sealink*, Ian Allan, Shepperton, 1982.

Haws, Duncan: *Merchant Fleets Britain's Railway Steamers*, TCL Publications, Hereford, 1994.

Henry, Fred: *Ships of the Isle of Man Steam Packet Co. Ltd*, Brown, Son & Ferguson Ltd, Glasgow, 1977.

Hodgson, F. M.: *West Coast of Scotland Pilot*, Hydrographic Department, Lords Commissioners of the Admiralty, London, 1958.

Holme, Richard: *Cairnryan Military Port*, G.C. Book Publishers, Wigtown, 1997.

Ian Allan ABC series: various titles and editions.

Kelly, Peter: 'Finished with Engines' in *Best of British*, March 1998, Stamford.

Liddle, Laurence: *Passenger Ships of the Irish Sea 1919-1969*, Colourpoint, Newtownards, 1998.

Longbottom, K.: 'Liverpool Riverside Station' in *Railway Magazine*, June 1950, London.

Luxton, J.H.: Mersey and Irish Sea Shipping at http://www.merseyshipping.co.uk/ .

McCall, Bernard: *Coasters Around Britain*, McCall, Barry, 1989.

MacHaffie, Fraser G.: *The Short Sea Route*, T. Stephenson and Sons, Prescot, 1975.

McNeil, D. B.: Coastal *Passenger Steamers and Inland Navigations in the South of Ireland*, Belfast Transport Museum, Belfast, 1965.

McNeil, D. B.: *Irish Passenger Steamship Services Volumes 1/2*, David & Charles, Newton Abbot, 1969 and 1971.

Murphy, Michael and Laura: *The Ocean Ferryliners of Europe Vol. 1 The Northern Seas*, David & Charles, Newton Abbot, 1987.

National Maritime Museum: *The Denny List Vols. 1-4*, National Maritime Museum, London, 1976.

Norden, Greg: *Landscapes Under the Luggage Rack*, GNRP, Bugbrooke, 1997.

Osborne, Brian D., Quinn, Iain and Robertson, Donald: *Glasgow's River*, Lindsay Publications, Glasgow, 1996.

Parsons, David A.: *Ships Seventy One*, Ian Allan, Shepperton, 1970.

Price, M. R. C.: *The Pembroke and Tenby Railway*, Oakwood Press, Oxford, 1986.

Ripley, Don and Rogan, Tony: *Designing Ships for Sealink*, Ferry Publications, Kilgetty, 1995.

Shepherd, John: *The Life and Times of the Steam Packet*, Ferry Publications, Kilgetty, 1994.

Ships Monthly, Burton on Trent, many issues.

Sim, Duncan: 'Boat Train To Riverside' in *Railway Magazine*, November 1971, London.

Sinclair, Robert C.: *Across the Irish Sea*, Conway Maritime Press, London, 1990.

Walker, Fred: *Song of the Clyde*, W.W. Norton & Co., London. 1984.

Widdows, Nick: *Car Ferries of the British Isles 1992/93*, Ferry Publications, Narberth, 1992.

Widdows, Nick: *Ferries of the British Isles & Northern Europe*, Ferry Publications, Narberth, 1998.